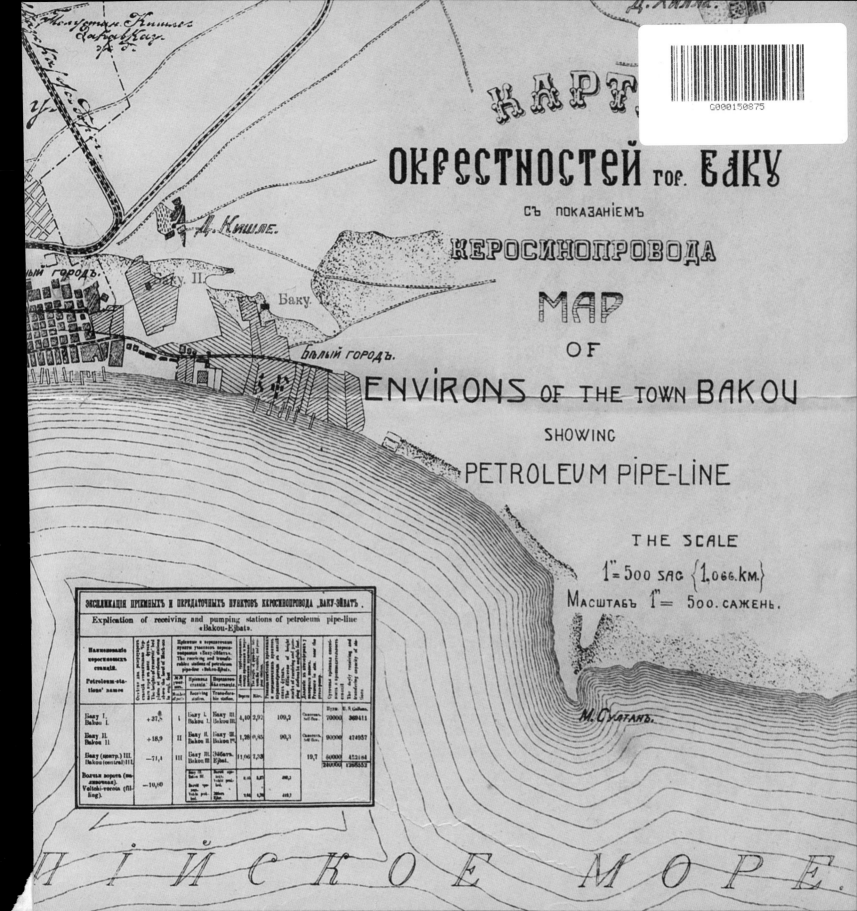

MEMORIES OF BAKU

Memories of Baku

EDITED BY

Nicolas V. Iljine

MARQUAND BOOKS, SEATTLE

Baku postcard, "Greetings from Baku."

SFERIQ

This book is published with the support of Ulvi Kasimov, the head of the investment company SFERIQ.

We thank Elyar Damirov and his family for their support.

Postcard with view of Bailov Cape, Baku.

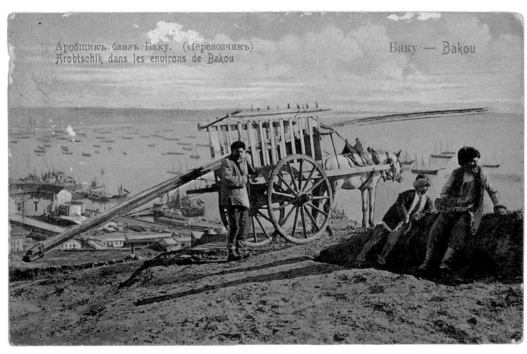

Cart driving men near Baku.

Postcard: "Greetings from Baku."

Poster for "Northern Wine" from the D.Z. Saradzev Winery, Baku, 1910, by I.M. Mashistova, Moscow.

Azeri Mosque.

A leaf from the album "Scenes, Landscapes, Customs and Costumes of the Caucasus. Drawn from nature by Prince Gregory Gagarin," Paris, 1847.

Camels in the Square, Baku.

Waterfront Promenade.

View of Old City from outside the fortress walls, 1888.

Table of Contents

Баку Васои
Набережная Имп. Александра II.
Quai Alexandre II.

Quay Alexander II.

Крѣпостная стѣна — Le rempart   Баку — Васоu

Изданіе О. Оруджова съ Братьями, Телефонная, Баку

The Ramparts.

"Guide to Baku," ed. Valentin Serov, Baku, 1924.
Handbook for the Baku Fair in 1924.

Street view of Baku.

Preface

Nicolas V. Iljine

——————
——————

Over the last few years I have traveled to Baku eighteen times and have been fascinated by this multifaceted ancient city on the shores of the Caspian Sea, by the richness of its cultural traditions, and by the hospitality and warmth of its people, which remain unparalleled.

I was privileged to meet the president and the first lady of Azerbaijan, as well as artists, musicians, writers, actors, architects, students, ministers, and wealthy businessmen.

Encounters with lively market scenes in Baku and with simple workers and farmers in the picturesque countryside surrounding the capital enhanced our colorful impressions.

What originally started as a modest collection of old Baku postcards gradually turned into a passion for discovering more and sharing these impressions with friends and others further afield. Thus, my museum colleague Mary Hannah Byers and I decided to embark on this book with the help of knowledgeable writers and the enthusiastic support of many newly won friends in Baku. Special thanks to Hannah Byers for her help and advice during the initial phases of this project.

In the 1990s, I read the Russian version of "The Bygone Days" (*Dni minuvshie*), in which the late Manaf Suleymanov describes the rise from rags to riches and the fall back to rags of one of Baku's famous oil barons, Zeynalabnin Taghiev (1838–1924), and the already legendary romantic novel *Ali and Nino* by Kurban Said. The spell of the period depicted in these novels awakened my interest in this country full of contrasts, a country that has changed its alphabet three times over and was home to an astonishingly liberal, satirical illustrated weekly journal, *Mollah Nasreddin*, which was published in Baku from 1922 to 1931.

In this book we tried to go beyond the classical stereotypes, such as "The Land of Fire" or "Baku, the Pearl of the Caspian" and focus instead on what we thought were the formative elements of today's cultural scene by looking back through the years up until the mid-1920s. So, admittedly, I have dwelt in nostalgia and have left the Soviet period and the phenomenally dynamic development of Azerbaijan and its capital, Baku, since Azerbaijan's independence in 1991 to more qualified historians and chroniclers.

Firstly, we are greatly indebted to our authors but also to many friends and supporters, the foremost being Fatma Abdullazade, Akif Abdullayev, Farkhad Akhmedov, Leyla Aliyeva, Elena Barkhatova, Antonina Bouis, Jean-Claude Bouis, Elena Chinyaeva, Roger Conover, Elyar Damirov, Chingiz Farzaliev, Fakhraddin Gurbanov, Abulfas Garaev, Suad Garaeva, Mikhail Gusman, Vasily Istratov, Ulvi Kasimov, Farkhad Khalilov, Pavel Khoroshilov, Thomas Krens, Olivier Mestelan, Georgy Putnikov †, Chingiz Qajar, Aidan Salakhova, Elchin Safarov, Mikhail Shwydkoi, Amanda Singer, and Maarif Teymur.

Because there is a wealth of literature about Baku in Azeri and in Russian, we thought that English would be the appropriate language in which to present this album in hopes of whetting the appetite for traveling to this vibrant city in the heart of the Caucasus on the Silk Road between Europe and Asia.

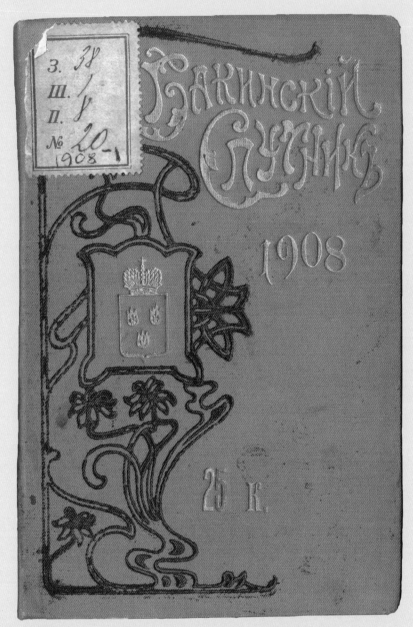

"Baku Satellite" Almanac, 1908.

Meditation in the Mosque on the Eve of the Schachsei-Wachsei Festival.

Общій видъ. Бульвара. Баку.

General view of the boulevard.

Camels on Nizami Street with a view of the Opera House designed by N. V. Bayev, 1910–11.

Europe Outside the Fortress Walls

Fuad Akhundov

———

THE EVENTFUL HISTORY OF BAKU, particularly that part of the city that lies outside of the Old City's fortress walls, is likened to an intricate, colorful portrait made in oil. Built at the time of the oil boom (1872–1920), this part of the city was imbued with a heavy mixture of European and Asian lifestyles, traditions, and architecture. This was the era in which the incredible fortunes of the local new rich, who were fueled by the desire to display their opulence and power, were manifested in the construction of the magnificent mansions so emblematic of oil-boom Baku. To give a better understanding of the background and history of this era, the events surrounding the first oil rush are briefly outlined in the pages that follow.

Crude oil had been produced in and around Baku since time immemorial. The earliest accounts of the city's oil production, given by Arab travelers such as Al Massoudi and Al Istakhri in the ninth and tenth centuries, tell of hand-dug pits. Oil extracted in this fashion was transported in wineskins by camel caravan and used primarily for household illumination.

By the time Baku was taken over by the Russian Empire in 1806, some one hundred wells were in operation. These wells became nationalized property at the time of the first peace treaty between Russia and Persia in 1813. Given the lack of private enterprise, low industrial demand, and heavy-handedness on the part of the new administration, production steeply declined. By 1820 the state decided to rent oil fields to private entrepreneurs. However, the very short leases offered (four years, followed by state repossession) hardly inspired many of the so-called oil farmers. Only in 1872, following substantial reforms in the Russian Empire, was this system abolished.

These new concessions in Baku's oil industry were comparable to letting a genie out of a bottle. Oil production was sixty times greater than it had been at the end of the first decade of the oil boom, and by 1901 the small city of Baku, with only 120,000 residents, provided over 51 percent of the world's output in crude oil. The oil boom had a truly explosive effect on the city's population. The population of the tiny ancient Old City, which in 1872 was encircled by double rampart walls and claimed a population of 15,000 residents, had by 1903 exploded into a town of 143,000 that proceeded to double in size during each decade that followed.

Needless to say, this unprecedented population growth resulted in an ethnic and cultural diversity that became a feature of Baku for decades to come. For example, in 1913, the last year of accurate statistics prior to World War I, out of 215,000 Bakuvians, there were 76,000 Russians; 71,000 Azeris; 41,000 Armenians; 10,000 Jews; 4,000 Georgians; 3,200 Germans; 2,300 Tatars; 1,700 Poles; and 1,300 Lezghis.[1] Although several of these ethnic groups are represented by a relative few, it was nonetheless possible to speak of a true phenomenon of Jewish physicians, German technicians, and, last but not least, Polish architects.

1. *Baku and Its Environs* (in Russian). Editor M. S. Shapsovich.

Baku Train Station, 1887.

Shirvanshakh Palace in the old city, 1887.

An urban landscape previously dominated by minarets was now dotted with Orthodox and Apostolic churches, Catholic and Lutheran cathedrals, and a beautiful synagogue located in downtown Baku that was donated by the local municipality in the early 1900s. Whatever the rationale behind this gift, it was not, as some have alleged, to reveal the number of Jews living in this now infamous Pale of the Settlement introduced by the anti-Semitic imperial authorities.[2]

The enormous influx of a very diverse population accounted for the rapid growth of the city outside of the original fortress walls. The Old City, with its meager twenty-two hectares (54.36 acres) of land and not a single straight street, was obviously incapable of absorbing the seemingly endless wave of newcomers attracted by the promising opportunities offered by the oil boom. Fortunately, the Inner City (Icheri Sheher) was miraculously preserved, thanks to its twelfth-century rampart, which remained intact. However, the town's seventeenth-century outer wall was dismantled in the early 1880s, and the Outer City (Bayir Sheher) began growing from that point on. An expressive and eloquent description of the two different cultures within this one city can be found in Kurban Said's novel *Ali and Nino,* a story of love between an Azeri nobleman and a Georgian princess, a Muslim and a Christian, at the time of the Russian Empire:

> There were really two towns, one inside the other, like a kernel in a nut. Outside the Old Wall was the Outer City, with wide streets, high houses, its people noisy and greedy for money. This Outer City was built because of the oil that comes

2. SHVUT. *Jewish Studies of South-Eastern Europe.*

from our desert and brings riches. There were theaters, schools, hospitals, libraries, policemen and beautiful women with naked shoulders. If there was shooting in the Outer City, it was always about money. Europe's geographical border began in the Outer City.

In fact, the fortress wall provided a sort of geographical, cultural, and architectural cleavage between Asia and Europe within Baku. While inside the wall Baku was still a dormant Oriental fort, outside the wall it was a bustling town often compared to American cities in its scale and pace of growth. This outer town, where people were "noisy and greedy for money," was laid out and planned by civil servants of the new Russian administration, whose representatives were at times as diverse as the city's population itself.

The Municipal Council (Gorodskaya Duma) was established in Baku in 1870 as part of the general reforms taking place in the Russian Empire. Several of the council's first high-ranking officials left an indelible imprint on the city's image and architecture, including Nicholas von der Nonne, a gifted architect and engineer of German extraction, who drafted one of the first plans for Baku outside of the citadel, and Stanislav Despot-Zenovich, a famous local figure of Polish descent who was the city's longest-standing mayor, having held office for sixteen years.

The influence of the Russian administration can be traced not only in the layout of the streets and avenues outside of the citadel but also in their original names: Alexandrovskaya Naberezhnaya (Alexander Quay), Nikolayevskaya (Nicholas Street), Velikhoknyazhesky Prospect (Grand Duke Avenue), Stanislavskaya (St. Stanislav Street), Olginskaya (St. Olga Street), Mariinskaya (St. Mary Street),

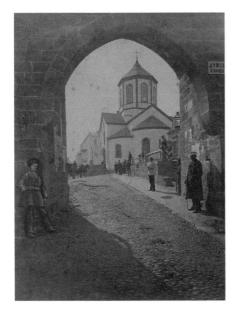

Christian church seen from the fortress gates, 1887.

Minaret of the Khan Mosque, Baku, 1887.

Горящія буровыя вышки и нефтяной фонтанъ   Баку.
Les fontaines de naphte en flammes.   Bakou.

Fountains of crude oil in flames.

and Merkuryevskaya (Mercury Street). All of these streets were renamed several times during the Soviet and post-Soviet periods, as a result of the turbulent social and political changes in the area. However, despite the streets' new names, their old architecture speaks eloquently of the past.

Architectural Wonders of Oil-Boom Baku

The architectural legacy of the first oil boom is one of the most remarkable assets of today's Baku. The charm of Baku's pre-Soviet architecture can best be grasped when several factors are borne in mind. The incredible fortunes resulting from early oil production met with the deeply rooted urban culture of the Inner City. Although it was moderate in size, the Old City had a centuries-old tradition of masonry, particularly stone carving. The magnificent stonework of the Shirvan-shah's Palace and the mosques of the Old City are clear evidence of this.

According to widespread lore, Baku's stonemasons were born with chisels in their hands. In truth, the limited choice of construction materials in the desertlike surroundings of Baku forced the local artisans to make the most of virtually the only building material to which they had access: the famous Baku limestone (sandstone). At the same time, Islamic tradition, with its ban on figurative art, channeled the creative impulses of the local stonemasons toward elaborate decoration. But, as intricate and ornate as these decorative elements were, they could no longer please the newly emerging oil tycoons, with their European preferences.

To furnish Baku's new wealth with the European architectural styles it demanded, Italian stonemason A. Franzi was invited to the city to train local masons to carve figures and faces from sketches that he made on paper. Franzi's know-how had a truly revolutionary effect on the plastic art of sculptural decoration. Human and animal images, gargoyles, imaginary and mythical creatures, and all sorts of symbolic figures became an integral part of the decorations on the facades of Baku's mansions of the late nineteenth and early twentieth centuries.

In fact, the architecture of oil-boom Baku boasts a certain advantage over that of a number of European cities in terms of its unusual and striking decorative stonework. Architectural elements that were plastered or molded in Europe were carved and hewn into stone in Baku, imbuing their structures with a greater sense of permanence and monumentality.

Architect Constantin Scurevich, circa 1900s.

Local oil barons were the dominant force in building the oil-boom Baku. Their incredible fortunes, coupled with the desire to show off and demonstrate their power, transformed the streets outside of the fortress wall into a kind of contest arena, where each mansion was built to surpass the last. Baku became an attractive destination for young and gifted architects. Graduates of the Institute of Civil Engineers in Saint Petersburg, such as Joseph V. Goslavski, Joseph K. Ploshko, and Ziver-bek Ahmedbekov, could find no better venue for carrying out their fantastical and bold creative endeavors than rapidly growing Baku, with its windfall money, ambitious clientele, plentiful and excellent local workforce, and, last but not least, lenient municipal authorities. This latter element explains several important features of pre-Soviet Baku in addition to its ornate stonework.

First, the architecture of Baku's oil-boom period is very mixed in terms of style. This diversity is explained by the fact that the outer town was built by the nouveaux riches, many lacking a basic education although striving to outdo one another. Hence, if one erected a mansion in the neoclassical style, the next would add baroque or art nouveau elements or Oriental motifs. The owner might not even know the names of the styles used in building his home—a hypothetical order from an oil magnate to an architect in those days might read something like, "I want to have an entrance like in Taghiyev's house, the dome like in Mukhtarov's mansion, the porch like in Dadashov's domicile, the decorations like in Mitrofanov's residence, and something of my own."

Another interesting feature of many of Baku's pre-Soviet mansions is that the homes feature an overt, even challenging individualism that is emblematic of their eras and their self-made owners. The elegance and aristocratic bearing of Isa-bek Hajinski, a high-born oil tycoon and well-known public figure, is matched perfectly with his flamboyant and elaborate palace on the sea front, just next to the Maiden Tower. On the other hand, stocky and corpulent Dmitri Mitrofanov, a Penza-born entrepreneur who made a fortune in Baku's oil, is accurately reflected in the sturdy, monolithic design of his residence in nearby Akhundov Garden. This mansion is also known for its extremely elaborate stone-carved architectural decor. Finally, the stately image of Murtuza Mukhtarov's palace is a true reflection of its tough, proud owner.

The well-trained and dedicated architects and civil engineers of this period also played an important role in creating Baku. Men such as Joseph V. Goslavski, Ploshko, Kazimir B. Skurevich, Eugene J. Skibinski, Constantine A. Borisoglebski, Nikolai G. Bayev, and Ziver-bek Ahmedvekov managed to channel their wealth, resources, and ideas into civilized architectural forms. At the same time, the rapid pace of construction coupled with a lack of supervision on behalf of the municipal authorities resulted in a somewhat chaotic situation, in which a magnificent edifice could find itself standing amid ramshackle shanties.

While Baku's Azeri oil tycoons were engaging in one-upmanship, designing their houses in a Western manner, adorning them with sculptures, reliefs, and frescoes (the subject matter of which was strictly forbidden by their religion), some of Baku's European oil magnates erected their residences in a very opulent Eastern manner, such as the Rhylskys, a wealthy oil-baron family of Polish descent whose house is now known as the Azerittifaq Building. Of special note is the work of such architects as Konstantin Skurevich, Nikolai Bayev, and Eugene Skibinski, all of whom demonstrated a strong sensitivity toward local architectural traditions and used these traditions most effectively in their work.

Despite the ethnic diversity of Baku at the time of the oil boom, the outer part of the city was primarily built by local oil tycoons. Although Azerbaijanis comprised only 34 percent of the total population, they owned over 80 percent of the city's real estate. The Russian community accounted for 36 percent of the population yet owned only 6 percent of the city's real estate, while the Armenians, accounting for 19 percent of the population, controlled 11 percent of the real estate. Because Baku was technically a part of the Pale of the Settlement, the Jewish community tended not to own but rather to rent real estate from the local population. This fact alone meant that Baku's Jewish population was more accepting of the expropriation of property that came with Communism.

The richest Baku-based oil producers in the Russian empire, the Nobel brothers, concentrated their construction activities in oil production and refinement areas. Their magnificent Villa Petrolea, laid out amid the refineries of Black Town, was among Baku's first green areas and was built upon a landfill, with trees and water brought from the Volga River. The Nobel brothers built nothing in downtown

Baku. The Rothschilds' architectural legacy includes two fine buildings, now landmarks, which today house the general public prosecutor's office and the fine arts museum. The domiciles of the town's local wealthy families, including the Taghiyevs, the Naghiyevs, the Rzayevs, the Ashurbekovs, the Safaraliyevs, and the Dadashovs, formed the heart of Baku's downtown. As odd as it may seem, some of these families were not involved in the oil business at all.

Taken as a whole, the extraordinary mix of varied traditions and styles of pre-Soviet Baku made for an eclectic architecture. The unbridled imagination and extraordinary wealth of the local oil barons, coupled with the availability of highly trained and talented architects and stonemasons, gave the residences of this era a highly unique quality. These conditions eventually gave rise to the style one may call "the Baku Eclectic" that is still very much in evidence in today's downtown Baku.

The oil boom of 1872–1920 also had an enormous impact on the city's technical and cultural development. The world's first oil tanker, *Zoroaster*, built in 1879 and used by the Nobel brothers, was finally sunk by the Soviets in 1949 to build a bridgehead for the first offshore platforms in the world, known as the Oil

Cartoon of H. Z. Taghiyev, 1901. Taghiyev in his gala uniform of the State Councilor receiving congratulations from all over the world upon foundation of his school for Muslim girls, the first secular institution of its kind in the Islamic world.

Rocks,[3] and was followed by the introduction of cutting-edge technologies in oil production and refinement. Cultural developments included the founding of the first European theater (the Taghiyev Theater) in 1883, the staging of the first opera in the Muslim world (Uzeyir Hajibeyov's *Leyli and Majnun*) in 1908, and the first secular school for Muslim girls (the Taghiyev Girls' School) in 1901, to name just a few. In this regard, one of the most fascinating aspects of Baku's first oil boom was the cohort of extraordinary personalities associated with it who played an exceptional role in shaping the city's unique atmosphere.

Legacy of the Oil Barons

Baku's first oil barons were those who managed to amass incredible fortunes within a very short time frame. While the stories behind their newfound wealth were at times amazing, their personal lives were often characterized by hardship. Hardly any could be said to have been born with silver spoons in their mouths. Originally from poor families and often lacking in even rudimentary education, most had to fight their way to the top, toiling in oil fields and the like. Most succeeded in business only at an old age. The cultural and architectural legacy left behind by these self-made scions can still be felt in Baku today.

H. Z. Taghiyev

Hajji Zeynalabdin Taghiyev (1823–1924) stands out among Baku's early oil tycoons. Beyond his enormous fortune and obvious business acumen, he was noted for his outspoken philanthropy and daring exploits in education and the arts. Taghiyev's entrepreneurial spirit and willingness to invest in spheres unrelated to oil make him a role model for Azerbaijan today.

Like many of the early oil barons, Taghiyev was born to a poor family in the Old Town. His father was cobbler, and his mother died when he was only ten. His parents' illiteracy, coupled with the byzantine civil registration methods of the period, list Taghiyev's year of birth at anywhere from 1823 to as late as 1842. Quite possibly the records were tinkered with intentionally, upon the occasion of his second marriage to the much younger Sona Arablinskaya.

At the age of twelve, Taghiyev was apprenticed to a stone carver, and by the age of fifteen he was already considered a master craftsman. (Later, when he oversaw the embellishment of his own mansions, he would keep a close eye on the progress of the stonemasons.) Moving into construction, and later into kerosene, by 1872 his company was able to buy into the oil business as soon as the Russian government introduced concessions. In early 1878 a gusher was discovered on land that he owned, propelling his company to success. Several years later Taghiyev oversaw the annual production of around one million barrels of oil and

3. Mir-Yussif Mir Babayev, *Brief Chronology of the History of Azerbaijan's Oil Business, Baku*, 191.

ЗДАНИЕ ГОСПОДИНА ГАДЖИ-ЗЕЙНАЛАБДИН ТАГИЕВА.

TAGHIYEV PALACE
An old photograph of the exterior.

kerosene.[4] In a remarkable display of business acumen and foresight, Taghiyev sold his company to British entrepreneurs in 1897, just before Baku's oil production became too much for Russia to absorb and the market was glutted.

Wholly unaffected by the glutted market, Taghiyev was left only with the decision of how to spend the enormous fortune he made by selling his company. He decided to invest in diverse areas unrelated to oil, such as the nascent cotton trade in the region, shipping, and later electric power. Around the turn of the century, Taghiyev's electric company built two power plants, which he co-owned. One of the two is still operating, whereas substantial parts of the other have been renovated, reportedly for Baku's Jazz Center. By 1914 Taghiyev had expanded into banking, becoming one of the founding fathers of Baku's Merchants Bank. The Taghiyev Shopping Center (Taghievsky Passazh), erected downtown in 1896, remains among the best malls in Baku to this day.

4. Nardova, *Early Monopolies in Russian's Oil Industry,* 29 (in Russian).

Taghiyev's influence was felt profoundly in nearly all spheres of local enterprise. The idea of building up the non-oil sector of Azerbaijan, so strongly advocated by the country's current government, was first put into practice by an illiterate local oil baron over a century ago.

Taghiyev's philanthropic activities were unparalleled. In 1883 he founded the first European theater in Baku (now the Operetta Theater). Impeccably designed and furnished, the Taghiyev Theater staged the first opera in the Muslim world, *Leyli and Majnun,* in 1908. In 1912 the first Muslim opera singer, Shovket Mammadova, made her debut there. There was a vehement reaction to both events by local zealots, causing the main performers to flee the scene post-performance; nonetheless, the precedent was set. One-hundred years after Mammadova, the first European-style Muslim opera singer, was shot at by zealots in the Taghiyev theater, the city of Baku successfully hosted Europe's largest and most popular show, the Eurovision 2012.

Taghiyev also held a prominent city council seat, published *The Caspian* newspaper (one of the most widely read in the city), and founded several vocational schools and schools for girls. His concern over the provincial and isolated existence of Azeri women prompted him to take particular interest in their educational opportunities. Addressing a high-ranking Russian official who oversaw schools for the Caucasus region, Taghiyev wrote,

> The isolation of the Muslims and their alienation from Russian culture is supported by several dogmatic religious principles. . . . What constitutes the very stronghold of these pseudo-religious traditions is seclusion of the Muslim woman and her unawareness of her human rights. . . . What we need is to accomplish the comprehension of the Muslim woman of her inalienable human rights through primary education.[5]

As oddly prescient as it may seem, Taghiyev's statement was made fifty-two years before the adoption of the Universal Declaration of Human Rights, and was most likely dictated rather than written. Amazingly, Taghiyev's school project prevailed, although it had to walk a fine line between the concealed reluctance of tsarist authorities and the vehement resistance of several local clerics.

Radical mullahs exercised a great deal of influence on the populace and with almost Talibanic zeal blamed Taghiyev for infringing on Islamic traditions. Their arguments boiled down to the following: Our mothers and grandmothers never went to school, so why should our daughters? To put a stop to this, Taghiyev sent a valued supporter to visit one of nearby Persia's most powerful Shia leaders in order to get authorization to open the school. The authorization was duly obtained,

AGHA ISMAYIL NAGHIYEV, Mussa Naghiyev's only son.

5. "The Central State History Archive of the Republic of Azerbaijan," dossier (archive) 309, number 62, file 61, 47-48.

The first secular school for Muslim girls,
established by H. Z. Taghiyev. Designed by
J. V. Goslavski and built between 1986 and 1901.

Mourning in a family of a girl sent to
the Taghiyev School, as if she has been
sentenced to death.

STUDENTS OF THE TAGHIYEV SCHOOL
In their new uniforms modelled after Russian
schools (with German aprons), introduced in
1907 after Taghiyev sent his daughters to the
famous Smolny Girls Institute in St. Petersburg.

mainly due to lavish gifts presented to each religious leader concerned. However, the idea worked, and whenever any cleric in Baku accused Taghiyev of violating Muslim tradition, he would simply remind the cleric whose authorization lay behind the school.

At long last, on October 9, 1901, after more than five years in the attempt, the Taghiyev Girls' School was opened to great fanfare. This was the first secular school for girls of its kind anywhere in the Muslim world. The school's magnificent building, designed by Joseph Goslavski, one of old Baku's most renowned architects, today houses the Institute of Manuscripts at the Azerbaijan National Academy of Sciences.

Taghiyev's high-profile and well-publicized philanthropic endeavors saved him from being purged by the Communist regime once they took over in 1920. Quite uncharacteristically, he was "kindly allowed" to retain one of his homes for his own use until his death in 1924, when the rest of the family was evicted. His wife Sona Taghiyeva, who once had been one of Baku's most revered women, was found dead in the street in 1932, after a decade of beggary.

Agha Musa Naghiyev:
Architectural Legacy of the "Miserly" Oil Baron

Agha Mussa Naghiyev (1849-1919) was another very familiar name to Bakuvians at the turn of the twentieth century. Born to a poor peasant family in Bilajary, one of Baku's outskirting suburbs, Naghiyev managed to become the wealthiest Azeri oil baron of all time. Accumulating his fortune with bewildering speed, his company

STUDENTS OF THE TAGHIYEV
SCHOOL
In their original uniform based
on the traditional Caucasian girl
dress (1901–1907).

Embroidery class at the Taghiyev
School.

AGHA MUSSA NAGHIYEV (1849–1919), the richest and reportedly the stingiest Azeri oil baron, left the most marvelous architectural legacy in the city.

was incorporated in 1899 and by 1910 had reached an annual rate of production of one million barrels of oil a year. Despite Naghiyev's immense fortune and the continuing rapid growth of his business, he earned the reputation of being the most tight-fisted–if not the greediest–oil baron of his time. Several stories of his extreme parsimony evolved into legend.

As one such story goes, Naghiyev and his son Ismayil were invited to an evening party hosted by a local charitable society. Each guest was asked to make a donation to an orphanage, and the donations would be personally collected by leading society ladies. On that particular night, Sona Taghiyeva was presiding, the idea being that no one would dare to place a small sum of money on the tray held by such an illustrious and influential lady. This philosophy worked well with Naghiyev the younger, who placed a hundred-ruble banknote squarely in the middle of the tray, easily a month's salary for one of his field workers. When it came time for Naghiyev the elder to place his donation on the tray, he looked through all of his pockets and came up with a miserly three rubles. When those around him asked how he, the great Naghiyev, could donate such a meager sum after his son had donated one hundred rubles, he immediately retorted, with an angelic expression, "Oh my! My son is supposed to do that because of whose son he is. He's the son of a millionaire. But whose son am I? I'm the son of a poor peasant!"

Unfortunately, even the millions of this poor peasant's son could not save the life of his own son Ismayil, who succumbed to tuberculosis at a very young age. This event forever altered Naghiyev's attitude toward money, and the formerly miserly oil baron erected the city's largest hospital, which still bears his name today and only recently underwent a thorough renovation to become Azerbaijan's Ministry of Health. Naghiyev's hospital was the first institution to try to tackle infectious diseases in Baku. He went on to chair the board of trustees at the Baku Modern School and to found the Muslim Philanthropic Association, also known as the Ismailiye after Naghiyev's late son (at the time, "Muslim" connoted "Azeri"). The building took six years for the accomplished Polish engineer Joseph Ploshko to construct. Based on the Venetian Gothic style, the building is strikingly similar to the Ca D'Oro in Venice, and skillfully combines the Gothic and Oriental traditions with the impeccable stonework so typical of old Baku.

The same charitable foundation that had received three rubles from the stingy Naghiyev later received 350 golden rubles from him to commemorate the death of his beloved son. The foundation used the funds to construct an elaborate headquarters for themselves, and this building became the central hub for many Azeri philanthropic initiatives. Today the building houses the Azerbaijan National Academy of Sciences, and one would be hard-pressed to find another building as impressive in all of Baku.

These philanthropic institutions constitute only part of Naghiyev's architectural legacy. Always looking for ways to diversify his wealth, outside of crude oil production, Naghiyev prudently invested in rental housing throughout Baku, eventually becoming the largest landlord in the city. Today his buildings constitute the core of Baku's architectural legacy.

All of Naghiyev's buildings were designed by Joseph Ploshko and built by the Kasumov Brothers Construction Company, one of old Baku's most prominent construction companies. The Kasumov family business was run by three brothers: Hajji, Ali, and Imran. Born in Ordubad in today's Nakhichevan region, to a family engaged in producing dyes for carpet wool, the brothers moved to Baku in the late nineteenth century to get involved in the nascent building industry surrounding the oil boom. In short order they were handling brigades of skilled workers and craftsmen and had succeeded in landing many of the city's top construction projects.

Each of the Kasumov brothers was known for being a character. The oldest of the three, Hajji (1870-1937), was known for his passion and vigor and his shrewd entrepreneurial skills and was reputedly quite a Casanova. On the other hand, his brother Ali (1873-1943) was known as a balanced, pious, and sober man. For these reasons he handled the finances of the family business. And the youngest brother, Imran (1879-1914), was primarily involved in architectural decorations and embellishments. According to the recollection of Hajji's son, his father used to test the quality of the completed buildings by inserting the thin blade of a penknife between the stones of the facework, and God forbid if the blade passed through. It was this exceptional quality of work, so alien to Baku's current standards, that made the Kasumovs so successful. It came as no surprise to anyone that Mussa Naghiyev granted the brothers contracts for seven residential buildings between 1908 and 1910.

Today these seven buildings stand out among Baku's finest landmarks: the twin houses in the art nouveau style in front of the Nizami Cinema on May 28 Street (formerly Telefonnaya Street), the edifice adjoining the opera houses, and Mussa Naghiyev's former residence at the intersection of Nizami and Rasul Rza Streets (formerly Torgovaya and Mariinskaya Streets). Although there are many others, this latter building stands out as epitomizing the height of luxury and quality. Thus the "miserly" oil baron managed to leave an indelible impression on Baku's image and architecture.

There was one person to whom Naghiyev never begrudged any sum. As one might suspect, this was a woman—his second wife, Yelizaveta Grigoryevna. Although little evidence of her is left, beyond a captivating photo found in her husband's automobile, she was widely known for her beauty and charm and became the subject of local lore for decades.

Proud of his wife's charms, Mussa Naghiyev reportedly referred to her as "our wife" (*nash zhena* in Russian), incorrectly using the word *nash* ("our") in the masculine form. Making mistakes in Russian was no great surprise coming from an

Murtuza Mukhtarov (1859-1920)
A self-trained engineer, drilling wizard, and an oil magnate of old Baku.

THE MUKHTAROV MOSQUE
Located in Mukhtarov's home village of
Amirajan, it was erected between 1907–8
and designed by Z. Ahmedbekov.

oil tycoon who never had any formal schooling. However, such a form of address reminded everyone of the famous royal "we" used by the Russian monarchs of the day. As the story goes, Mussa Naghiyev was once asked, "Do you think you are Nicholas II to say 'our wife' instead of 'my wife'?" Naghiyev wittily replied, "If Nicholas has the same treasure, let him say 'our wife,' too."

While Mussa Naghiyeva was lucky enough to have passed away in 1919, only a year before the Communist takeover of Baku and the brutal expropriation of all his property, Yelizaveta was said to have ended up in desperate poverty under the Soviets.

Agha Murtuza Mukhtarov:
The "Tough Guy"

The name Agha Murtuza Mukhtarov (1855–1920) would undoubtedly figure into anyone's hagiography of oil-boom Baku. Like most of his peers, Mukhtarov was not born to privilege, nor did he have access to a formal education. Nonetheless, he managed to become a well-respected self-taught engineer and a "drilling-wizard" in pre-Soviet Baku. One of the tools he invented for the production of drill bits was referred to for decades as the "Mukhtarov tool"–despite the Communist authorities' official taboo against this term.

Mukhtarov was born to a poor family in the Baku suburb of Amirajan in either 1855 or 1859. One of the city's oldest suburban settlements, Amirajan was located in the immediate vicinity of oil-rich areas, such as Surakhany, Sabunchu, and Balakhany, and so Mukhtarov began toiling in the oil fields in his teens. A fit and robust young man, Mukhtarov was quick to handle any difficult job, yet he did not confine himself to simple digging and bailing. He was keen to grasp technical innovations and even introduced several new techniques. It was therefore hardly surprising that he was soon promoted to field technician and then manager, and finally, in his early thirties, Mukhtarov succeeded in founding a company that would eventually become one of the largest drilling enterprises in Baku. By 1910 this company, the Murtuza Mukhtarov Joint Stock Venture, was operating two mechanical plants, in Balakhany and Bibi-Heibat, with nearly 1,500 employees. Equipped with the most cutting-edge technologies of the day, the plants were producing a good quarter of all oil-field equipment used in Baku.

Mukhtarov had a number of characteristics that made him a successful businessman at a time when the intense oil rush had turned Baku into a kind of Wild West for budding entrepreneurs. Aside from his considerable hands-on experience and his outstanding technical gifts in the art of drilling, Mukhtarov displayed profound business acumen and was known for his ruthlessness when push came to shove. As stories went, Mukhtarov was at least partially responsible for rounding up local gangsters (*gochu*) and attempting to do away with local revolutionaries, including the man who later came to be known as Joseph Stalin.

Naturally, Mukhtarov looked to expand his business and did not restrict himself to Baku. His adventurous spirit got him actively involved in oil production in Grozny, making him a frequent visitor to the North Caucasus. It was one such trip that later proved pivotal.

While in Vladikavkaz, capital of North Ossetia, Russia, Mukhtarov was invited to a dinner by Akhmed Bey Tuganov, a retired general of the Russian army, who had heard much of the enterprising, tough, self-made oil magnate from Baku. The Tuganovs were one of the most esteemed local families. As the story goes, that night Mukhtarov was introduced to his host's daughters, one of whom, Liza, entranced him. Unsuccessful in his previous marriage, Mukhtarov was determined in his desire to marry an Ossetian princess. However, his request was met with polite refusal from the girl's parents, who declined based on Mukhtarov's social origins. Although impoverished, the highborn family was reluctant to forge ties with a rich oil magnate of such lowly background.

Infuriated by the refusal, Mukhtarov responded with an extraordinary gesture. He paved his way to the family's door by erecting a stately mosque on the bank of the Terek River. This iconic landmark, resembling the Mameluke mosques in Cairo, stands in Vladikavkaz to this day. Apparently, Mukhtarov dedicated the mosque to the Tuganov family, which served to increase their

LIZA MUKHTAROVA (NÉE TUGANOVA)
Murtuza Mukhtarov's spouse,
an Ossetian noblewoman and
one of the first ladies of old Baku.

RUBABA AND IMRAN KASSUMOV
A couple for whom the construction of the palace proved to be fatal. The inscription on the bottom reads: Passed Away: January 20, 1914 (for Imran) and February 11, 1914 (for Rubaba).

prestige in the surrounding community. The gesture left the family little room to hesitate, and so Mukhtarov brought his bride back to Baku in handsome style, accompanied by mounted escorts on white horses. Liza Tuganov arrived at Baku as a true princess and went on to become one of its most esteemed and revered first ladies.

Liza played a remarkable role in her husband's life. Mukhtarov had been a severe man, used to literally fighting his way through many a situation, although this was typical under his circumstances. But Liza managed to transform him into a true gentleman. Looking at Mukhtarov's photos, one would hardly guess that this elegant man was born to a family of poor peasants living on the outskirts of Baku. Fluent in Russian, Mukhtarov could also employ many expressions in English and French and was known as an adherent of British culture, hosting regular five o'clock tea parties and receptions.

The couple traveled to Europe together, particularly Italy, with great frequency. One of these trips had a lasting effect on Baku's image. While in Italy, Liza was astounded by the architecture of one of the Gothic palaces she saw. She shared her admiration with her husband, whose reaction was apparently quite restrained. Little did she or anyone suspect that Mukhtarov would use the design of that palace as a model for a residence he would build for her in Baku. Having purchased the plans and made a few modifications with the help of Joseph Ploskho, Mukhtarov constructed a copy of the palace in Persidskaya Street (now M. Mukhtarov Street) between 1911 and 1912. The remarkably short construction period and high quality of work was, as was often the case, owed to the Kasumov Brothers Company. Unfortunately, in this instance the construction proved fatal for the youngest brother, Imran.

The youngest of the Kasumov brothers, Imran was undoubtedly one of the most outstanding personalities of the whole clan. He was not only an excellent contractor but also a famous patron of the arts. Living in the immediate vicinity of Uzeyir Hajibeyov, the founding father of classical Azerbaijani music, Imran Kasumov let the largest hall of his residence be used for rehearsals for *Leyli and Majnun,* the first Muslim opera. As the staging of this opera was a rather bold step for its time, and no traditional rehearsal space could be used for fear of threats by local radicals, Kasumov's residence became their safe haven. Aside from supporting the actors, Imran was known for his melodic voice and performed one of the opera's key arias himself, acting under the artistic alias of Kengerlinski.

As with so many vivid personalities, our portrait of Imran Kasumov would be incomplete without mentioning his wife, Rubaba Kasumova (1882–1914), on whom he lavished enormous affection. With no children of their own, Imran and Rubaba were nonetheless one of the happiest couples in Baku. Their very lifestyle was an audacious challenge to the deeply rooted restrictions placed on women at that time. Although a confirmed Muslim, Kasumova dressed in fashions

MURTUZA MUKHTAROV WITH WIFE LIZA, circa 1910.

MUKHTAROV PALACE erected between 1911–12 in Baku by Murtuza Mukhtarov, reportedly as a gift for his wife who loved a similar palace in Italy.

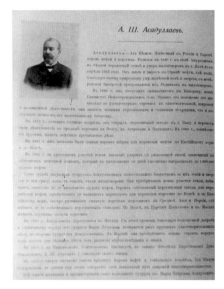

Biography of Agha Shamsi Asadullaev.

from Paquenne, one of the city's most fashionable emporiums. Kasumova would routinely appear sporting ostrich feathers (a cutting-edge style of the time, called *esprit*), while the majority of her countrywomen were still wearing veils.

Unfortunately, the idyll of Imran and Rubaba was short-lived. In a tragic twist of fate, their demise was bound to that of one of Baku's most famous landmarks—Mukhtarov Palace. Although the main construction of the palace was accomplished by 1912 in record-breaking time, several external decorative elements were still to be added, mainly an impressive stone statue of a medieval knight that crowned the entire composition.

On January 14, 1914, while attempting to install the statue of the knight from the steep pitch of the roof, using no supporting scaffolding, Imran Kasumov fell to his death at the age of thirty-five. The accident deeply shocked the city, which barely had time to recover before the suicide of Rubaba Kasumova was discovered twenty days later. According to her relatives' recollections, she reacted to her husband's demise saying: "After Imran's death," she told others, "I have two options: either to leave Baku forever or to go under the veil." Neither of these options seemed acceptable to the free spirit who passed away at the tender age of thirty-two.

Returning to the Mukhtarovs, the rapid construction of the palace was a complete surprise to Liza. As the story goes, when the building was nearly complete (although without the fatal statue of the knight), Murtuza Mukhtarov took his spouse for a stroll around downtown. As the couple turned onto Persidskaya Street, the freshly constructed palace was suddenly revealed. As the story goes, Mukhtarov feigned total surprise and innocently asked, "Darling, doesn't it remind you of something?" Liza was reportedly astounded, exclaiming, "It's the same palace I saw in Italy.... How could it simply appear in Baku? It's a fairy tale!" Mukhtarov's response was short and sweet: "I love you so much, dear, that I can make a fairy tale a reality for you. This is your home now."

As was the case with other oil tycoon families, the Communist takeover of Baku on April 28, 1920, turned into a horrible personal tragedy for the couple. Mukhtarov's tough stance on revolutionaries in earlier years made him an obvious target for the Soviet troops entering the city. Keenly aware of this reality, Mukhtarov nonetheless refused to flee Baku when reportedly urged to do so at one of his five o'clock tea parties as the Red Army was steadily approaching the city.

"I was born in this city to a poor family, and I have hard-earned everything I have—as long as I live, no barbarian will enter my home in soldier's boots," Mukhtarov was reported to state. Unfortunately, the Red Army soldiers did enter his palace—but on horseback. When Mukhtarov encountered them, he turned his gun on them and then on himself.

Later that same grim day, Liza Mukhtarova was thrown out of the palace. Deprived of virtually everything she had, she reportedly managed to escape Baku with a diplomat, only to be robbed by him upon their arrival in Istanbul. Suffering enormous hardship, she finally managed to make her way to Paris, which was at that time the hub of the Russian emigration. She died there in the 1950s, although her relatives never knew exactly when, as, due to the exigencies of the Cold War, there was no possibility of contacting her after World War II.

As for the gorgeous Mukhtarov Palace, odd as it may seem, between 1922 and 1937 it was used by Soviet authorities as a school for the elimination of illiteracy among Muslim women. During this time, thousands of Azeri women, many of them still sporting the traditional yashmak (*chador*), took up the pen for the first time in their lives.

More recently, the Mukhtarov Palace became Baku's main wedding hall (Palace of Happiness), where generations of Bakuvians, this writer among them, were officially married in the eyes of the state. As the home of two stories of beautiful though tragic love, what better venue for matrimonial bliss? Recently the building has undergone a substantial renovation with a part of it still reportedly to be used for marriage registration.

RUBABA AND IMRAN KASSUMOV

Agha Shamsi Asadullayev:
A Man Remembered for More than His Money

Agha Shamsi Asadullayev (1840-1913) stands out among the oil barons for his extraordinary generosity, charity, and aristocratic manner. Nevertheless, he shared the background of most of the self-made industrial tycoons of the time. Born to a poor family in the suburb of Amirajan, he received no formal education and began working in Baku's oil fields, first as a cart driver and then as a small contractor, before becoming a salesman at the Kokorev Oil Company.

Eager for entrepreneurial activity, Asadullayev established his own small oil business at the age of fifty, which flourished as a result of his previous experiences. Within a decade of its founding, Asadullayev's company was second only to Naghiyev's among native Azeri tycoons, and in the top fifteen of all of those operating in Baku.

Asadullayev was always keen to implement technical innovations and followed closely on the heels of the Nobel Company. While the Nobel brothers owned eighteen miles of oil pipeline, Asadullayev owned thirteen. The new oil tankers used by the Nobel company were named after prophets and scientific wizards—first was *Zoroaster,* then *Magomed, Moses, Bhudda, Spinoza,* and finally *Darwin.* Asadullayev followed suit by naming his similar tankers after the three As: *Africa, Asia,* and *America.* Asadullayev was an ambitious man, and his entrepreneurial activities stretched from Persia to Poland. He had offices, storage facilities, and oil distribution outlets scattered up and down the Volga, making a substantial network well known in Russia and beyond.

Meanwhile, Asadullayev's personal life was full of mishaps and travails. The major sources of his problems were his two wives. The first, Meyransa, was a typical

AGHA SHAMSI ASADULLAYEV (1840-1913)
One of Baku's most renowned oil tycoons and a recognized public figure highly esteemed all over the Russian Empire for his charity and benevolence.

ALI ASADULLAYEV
Shamsi's younger son, an adventurous
personality.

MEYRANSA ASADULLAEVA

Muslim woman with a strong aversion to the European innovations triggered by the oil boom and to the influx of foreigners it brought to Baku. Raised in the secluded and rigorous traditions of a Shia Muslim family, Meyransa tried her best to raise her three daughters in the same manner, despite the fact that times had changed irrevocably. Immediately upon marriage, each of the three daughters replaced her veil with the most fashionable dresses of the day, which they could well afford due to the fortunes of their father and their respective spouses. Speaking a bizarre mix of Russian and Azeri, the sisters found no better pastime than playing poker day and night. The same held true for the couple's two sons, Mirza and Ali. Educated, well mannered, handsome, and fashionable, the sons were guided by Islamic tradition only insofar as it did not hamper their lifestyle.

Needless to say, a woman of Meyransa's character and upbringing could hardly make a good match for Shamsi Asadullayev in Baku's beau monde. After having gained acceptance into high society, it came as no surprise that Asadullayev met a lady that would become his second spouse for years to come, Maria Nikolayeva. Rumors were told of her reportedly tainted past. Regardless, her beauty, manner, and intelligence won Asadullayev's heart. Had he kept her as a mistress, it would have caused his family no great distress in those days. However, Maria was too proud to accept this role, and she was not willing to become a second wife in a harem. Eventually, she issued the ultimatum: either me or your family.

Although Maria's ultimatum presented a tough dilemma to Asadullayev, who was firmly within middle age, with five grown children, he finally made his choice—he left his family for Maria, fully aware of the explosive reaction this would cause among his kin. A comparison of photographs of Asadullayev's two wives show a striking facial similarity, almost as if they were the same person dressed in Oriental and Western garments. It seems clear that Asadullayev's choice was not so much to do with Russian versus Azeri, Christian versus Muslim, or even Maria versus Meyransa. Rather, Asadullayev's choice was a matter of lifestyle—a modern European one—which would become imperative for his descendants. Although Meyransa bore the brunt of this decision, she remained the undisputed ruler of her own household, where she plotted her desperate revenge.

In the early 1900s, seemingly all of a sudden, the once-thriving Asadullayev family business appeared to be on the brink of a bankruptcy that was reportedly masterminded by Meyransa. As the story goes, one of the company's clerks "lost" an important telegram requesting a large shipment of crude to one of the Volga's river ports. When the product failed to be delivered, fines resulted for breach of contract. The initial warnings were also most likely "lost." By the time the matter became known to Asadullayev, the fees and interest had grown exponentially, putting his entire enterprise on the verge of ruin. Even offering his real estate and other assets as collateral could not secure a loan that would meet the snowballing amount of debt.

Brought up in a rigorously traditional Muslim household, their lifestyles changed
dramatically after marriage. Dressed in the most fashionable couture, they found
no better pastime than playing poker.

Anna Petrovna Asadullaeva, née
Nikolaeva
Shamsi's second and most beloved wife.

In this dreadful moment, salvation came from the most unlikely source: Baku's most miserly oil baron, Mussa Naghiyev. Very prudently, Asadullayev had married off his two handsome sons to the daughters of the other two richest oil barons, Naghiyev and Taghiyev. Notably, it was not the generous Taghiyev but the tight-fisted Naghiyev who paid Asadullayev's debt—perhaps the strongest argument against his reputation as a miser.

After the debt incident, Asadullayev managed a quick recovery, although his relations with his first wife and with most of his family were completely severed. He and Maria relocated to Moscow, where they became known for their charitable activities. Asadullayev donated one of his mansions to the Moscow Muslim community, and it remained the Tatar Center for decades. With no children of their own, the couple was broadly recognized for their support of local orphanages and asylums.

When the contents of Asadullayev's will became known, conflict with his family broke out again, as half of his assets, amounting to ten million rubles, was bequeathed to his second wife. Asadullayev's family and kin were furious and demanded reprisals. Aware of how harshly he would be judged, Asadullayev grew gravely concerned. Salvation came from Vladimir Gilyarovsky, a famous journalist who was friendly with Asadullayev's lawyer. Gilyarovsky managed to settle the quandary by adding a short amendment to the will reading, "In case of violent death of either my wife Maria or myself, I do hereby bequeath all my assets to the needs of charity." The amendment showed the wisdom of Solomon, for his kinsmen understood at once that five million rubles out of ten was better than nothing. In this way, those who had threatened the couple began guarding them with the utmost zeal.

The Asadullayevs' tremendous benevolence earned them a mention in the widely heralded *300 Years of the Reign of the Romanov Dynasty's Reign* published in 1913 to commemorate the history of the royal family. A general overview of the empire's most outstanding individuals was included. The Trades and Industries section listed several Azeri entrepreneurs. Asadullayev was the only one of those mentioned together with his spouse: "He was born and grew up in a country of oil where native wit accompanied with strong will and energy produce millionaires overnight." Maria Asadullayev was mentioned as a "woman of rare physical and spiritual beauty." Together, the couple were said to be "two giants of human spirit and geniuses of thought that came together to confront the hardships of life."

Regretfully, the year 1913 was to be the last for Asadullayev, who passed away in Yalta on April 21. The funeral for what had become one of Baku's most renowned oil tycoons turned into an immense mourning procession. Local villagers literally carried his body in their arms for over ten miles to the nearest train station to express their collective appreciation for all that Asadullayev had done for the Crimean Tatars. A crowd of no less than ten thousand awaited the train that

TEYMUR-BEK ASHURBEKOV
A hereditary nobleman whose land in Sabunchu was found to be full of oil during the first oil boom.

SARA'S BIRTHDAY AND CHRISTMAS PARTY
The Ashurbekov house, January 1914, with children of various ethnic origins. The third boy from the right in the third row is Lev Nussimbaum, the assumed author of the novel *Ali and Nino*.

bore his body to Baku. The more than three thousand employees of Asadulla-yev's company refrained from work for several days to mourn the loss of their beloved founder.

Despite all of the accolades and Asadullayev's very public burial, ironically, the exact location of his grave was lost when the Soviets turned the site into the Kirov Park and Recreation Center. Today the place is known as Martyrs Alley, with graves of the victims of the Soviet's invasion of Baku in 1990 and of the recent war in Karabakh.

Subsequent generations of the Asadullayev family were subjected to arrests and various forms of persecution under the Communists, forcing them to leave Baku in 1920. One of Shamsi Asadullayev's granddaughters, Banine (1905–1992), became a recognized émigré author in Paris. Her novels, *Caucasian Days* and *Parisian Days,* provide an excellent narrative of one of the richest Baku oil baron families in the context of turbulent historical events and the permanent exile that followed.

The once magnificent residence of the Asadullayev family at 9 Gogol Street was expropriated by the Soviets, neglected for more than eight decades, and has at last undergone extensive renovation. The impressive monogramatic *A* still beautifully adorns the entranceway and remains an emblem of one of the most generous and aristocratic oil tycoons of old Baku.

HAJI KASSUMOV
The eldest brother, the Casanova.

IMRAN KASSUMOV
The patron of the arts who fell to his death from
Mukhtarov Palace.

ALI KASSUMOV
The middle brother, a serious person.

TEYMUR-BEK ASHURBEKOV AND WIFE TUTU-KHANUM

ISMAT ASHURBEKOV
With her children in Tyrol, Austria, circa 1912.

28 GOGOL STREET
The residential house of the Ashurbekovs, built as a marriage gift by Teymur-bek Ashurbekov for his son and daughter-in-law. Designed by Joseph Goslavski, 1904.

The Ashurbekov Noble Family

In the late nineteenth and early twentieth centuries, the Ashurbekov family was greatly respected in Baku. They became oil barons but were of an old noble family whose roots in Baku could be traced back to the times of Nadir Shah, the early eighteenth-century Persian ruler. Nadir Shah bequeathed several villages on the Absheron Peninsula to his cousin, Ashur-khan Afshar, the founder of the local dynasty.

With the Russian takeover of Baku in 1806, the descendants of Ashur-khan assumed the family name Ashurbekov, based on their ancestral name, the title *bek,* meaning "feudal lord," and the Russian suffix *ov,* standing for "the sons." As owners of the large landed estates in Sabunchu, one of the most oil-rich outskirts of Baku, many representatives of the family became oil magnates during the first oil boom. However, it was their deeply rooted tradition of charity and philanthropy that gave the Ashurbekovs their extraordinary popularity. Two of the city's largest mosques, Taza Pir and the Blue Mosque, were erected by Nabat-khanum and Haji Ajdar-bek Ashurbekov, respectively.

Teymur-bek Ashurbekov was another member of the family who started his own oil business, later successfully developed by his two sons, Ali-bek and Bala-bek. His magnificent edifice at 28 Gogol Street is considered among the most valuable of Baku's architectural treasures to this day. In fact, this building was simply a marriage gift from Teymur-bek to his youngest son and daughter-in-law.

As the story goes, while visiting Tbilisi, the capital of Georgia, Teymur-bek Askhurbekov grew enchanted with the twelve-year-old niece of his good friend, a well-known local antique and carpet dealer. The good friends decided to become relatives by marrying their children. This practice of prearranged marriage was a common way for rich and influential families to maintain acceptable family lines. The young people simply waited until they were of marriageable age. Needless to say, the feelings of the young people were oftentimes neglected.

The dynamic worked differently in the case of Bala-bek Ashurbekov and Ismat Sultanov. The Sultanovs did not repudiate the idea of marriage, but as an advanced and modern family they did not want to give their girl to a "high-born ignoramus." For this reason, Bala-bek traveled to Tbilisi, then an administrative center of the South Caucasus, to study at one of the local high schools, taking classes in economics. This training proved helpful in running the family business for years to come. The major benefit of Bala-bek's stay in Tbilisi was that he was admitted to the Sultanov family and got to meet his fiancée, although meeting before the ceremony was contrary to the marriage traditions of the day. However, in this couple's case, meeting in advance worked well, as they fell sincerely in love with each other.

Encouraged by such a lucky coincidence and love match, Teymur-bek Ashurbekov determined to build a mansion in Baku that would be a "worthy place for a lady from Tiflis [Tbilisi]." According to recollections of his granddaughter Sara

JOSEPH GOSLAVSKI, Rastrelli of the Caucasus, with his family.

ARCHITECT JOSEPH GOSLAVSKI AND FAMILY

ALI-BEY ASHURBEKOV

Ashurbeyli, a recognized local historian in the Soviet period, he hired the outstanding architect Joseph Goslavski, who, although suffering from tuberculosis, came up with a beautiful neoclassical design for the dwelling. Completed in early 1904, the Ashurbekov residence, along with the City Hall (the BakSoviet), became the swan song of an architect otherwise known as the Caucasian Rastrelli.

The rich and ostentatious wedding of Bala-bek and Ismat Ashurbekov was lavishly celebrated, first in Tbilisi and then in Baku, where the newly married couple was presented with the gorgeous palatial building that was to be their home. Bala-bek added his own personal touch to the building's grandeur by commissioning frescoes for the main entrance. Happily, the frescoes survive to this day, and the entire entryway has been meticulously renovated by its current resident—sadly, a nearly singular exception in Baku at present.

This mansion housed several generations of the Ashurbekov family. The ground floor functioned as the family's company office. Bala-bek Ashurbekov's family resided in a twelve-room apartment on the upper floor. Here, as in many Azeri families, the matriarch—in this case Teymur-bek's wife, Tutu-khanum, the grandmother—played a critical role. A formidable woman and strongly opposed to European innovation, Tutu-khanum was said to have covered her hand with her sleeve when her granddaughters came to kiss her hand good night, as she considered them "impure." Her descendants recall her tremendous influence on her husband, which was probably the reason he never took a second wife, unlike many of his kin. Upon Teymur-bek's death, she had his remains transported to the holy site of Karbala in present-day Iraq, where she erected a stately tomb and hired a caretaker to tend his grave. Tutu-khanum managed to survive the turmoil of later periods and died at the age of nearly one hundred.

Meanwhile, Bala-bek Ashurbekov and his Georgian wife Ismat became key figures in the family. Their love endured, and they had six children. Bala-bek was a results-oriented type and a successful entrepreneur. Unlike most of his highborn relations, he personally oversaw his oil-rich estates and the installation of twenty-four rigs there that generated a substantial income. Ismat Ashurbekov possessed a unique blend of Oriental and European style. Fond of the latest modern fashions, she was also a connoisseur of traditional Azeri costumes, with a special preference for those of the Karabakh region. Extremely well educated, Ismat was fluent in Russian, had a passion for Persian poetry, and saw to it that her children were taught by French governesses and German tutors.

The Ashurbekov residence became a famous gathering place, particularly known for its annual Christmas party and frequent masquerade balls. A surviving photo of one of these New Year's parties, dating to approximately 1914, depicts the entire ethnic and cultural diversity of Baku at the time, with children of various origins enjoying a masked ball. One of these children was Lev Nussimbaum, the assumed author of *Ali and Nino* under the pseudonym Kurban Said.

In later years the five Ashurbekov girls, Sara, Sitara, Miriam, Adelya, and Nazima, would often look back and cherish the fond memories of their childhood in a city that seemed to them the Paris of the Caucasus. Their only brother, Rishad, was born in 1910 to the same life of prosperity and luxury. Each summer the children would travel together with their mother to one of the spas in Germany or Austria, where Sara once won a child beauty contest in 1913. These were the last years of tranquility and peace for the Ashurbekovs, as well as for all those of their milieu.

World War I, followed by revolution and ethnic bloodshed in Baku, put an end to the luxurious lifestyles typified by oil-boom Baku. During bloody events in March 1918 provoked by the Bolshevik and Dashnak (Armenian nationalist) government of the day, the Ashurbekov residence was attacked, and the family was forced to seek refuge in their home village of Sabunchu. Their city apartment was saved due to the cool-headedness of the French governess, Janette Greilot, who reportedly placed a tricolor at the main entrance, presenting the home as a diplomatic mission. However, the apartments of Ali-bek Ashurbekov on the other side of the house were brutally plundered. The family was allowed to

ISMAT ASHURBEKOV WITH ELDEST DAUGHTER, SARA
In Oriental garments.

BALA-BEY ASHURBEKOV

return to their house six months later, when Baku was released by Turkish and Azeri troops.

The house was thoroughly restored and renovated by Bala-bek, although the family was able to enjoy it for only a year before the Communists finally expropriated it in April 1920. For more than seventy years afterwards, the Ashurbekov sisters were unable to set foot onto their patrimonial estate. Ali-bek Ashurbekov was mistakenly arrested as one of his relatives, incarcerated, and sentenced to death. When the mistake was sorted out and he was let out of jail nearly a year later, he was clearly a changed man. The photos taken before and after his arrest attest to the horrible physical and psychological ordeal he had undergone.

Bala-bek Ashurbekov and his family immigrated to Turkey. For the next five years they stayed in Istanbul, where, according to Sara's recollections, the family enjoyed a sufficient lifestyle. The girls studied at the College of Jeanne D'Arc, and the son, Rishad, attended the prestigious university of Galatasaray. Having left the family's main sources of income behind in Baku, Bala-bek and Ismat liberally sold off the gems, jewelry, and other items of value that they had been able to take with them to support themselves during these years.

Bala-bek was beginning to get nostalgic for Baku when one day a letter arrived from his brother reporting the positive changes brought about by the New Economic Policy (NEP). The letter prompted the family's repatriation. The fatal outcomes of this decision would become apparent only several years later. By the early 1930s the NEP was over, and Bala-bek found himself arrested. The "grave charges" against him were obtained by an undercover investigator who had infiltrated Bala-bek's cell and provoked him into speaking against the authorities. Bala-bek was executed in 1935, and his older brother died from a heart attack in 1940.

For many years Sara and her siblings were stigmatized as "children of an enemy of the people." A graduate of the State University of Baku, Sara was fired from several teaching positions on the grounds of her "unreliable social origins." Only after Stalin's death in 1953 did she and her four sisters gain recognition for their contributions to the fields of medieval history, French, geology, medicine, and architecture, respectively.

The most tragic fate was borne by Rishad. A graduate of the medical department of the University of Baku, he could not bear the social stigma of being a child of an enemy of the people. During World War II, he volunteered to go to the front as a medical officer and was killed in Hungary in 1944. However, his sisters never dared to show the death notification to their mother. Because hundreds of thousands of people were missing after the war, Ismat Ashurbekov waited for her son to return for over ten years. She died in March 1954, still cherishing a hope, however small, that her son remained alive. Even when she was on her deathbed, her daughters could not bring themselves to tell her the truth.

Николаевская улица.   Rue Nicolas.

Баку.   Bakou.

Карабахская татарка.
Fille tartare de Karabak.

Nicholas Street and Tatar girl from Karabakh.

It took the surviving sisters nearly seventy-five years to revisit their family home at 28 Gogol Street in January 1995, together with a team of Dutch filmmakers who were shooting a story on the offspring of local noble families. The four ladies, the youngest in her mid-eighties, arrived to find the place completely dilapidated. In recent years the house has been thoroughly renovated, but, regretfully, no family member was alive to see it.

Nearly every beautiful mansion in the outer part of Baku could bear witness to a family story similar to that of the Ashurbekovs. Built at the time of Baku's rapid growth, these homes witnessed only a brief period of prosperity before the coming of the revolution, followed by ethnic clashes and bloodshed in 1918, expropriation and neglect under the Soviets, and a rapidly changing environment today that is generally unfavorable to historical preservation, leading us to the sad conclusion:

Baku is the place where every stone
Has a story of its own
And the stories could be magic
Were they only not so tragic. . . .

52

Theatre, Le Phenomene.

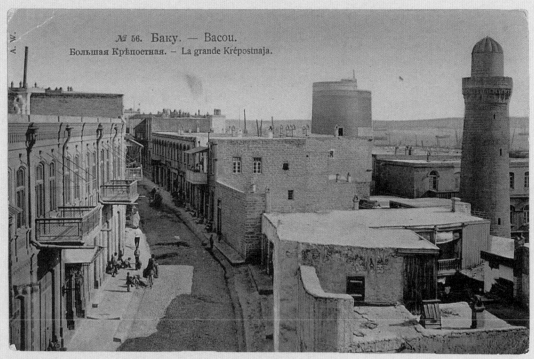

The Grand Krepostnaja.

BALA-BEK AND ISMAT ASHURBEKOV
"In love forever."

SARA ASHURBEKOV
Earliest photograph, circa
1906. She would later become
a famous historian.

MIRIAM ASHURBEKOV
The third daughter who later
would become a geologist,
circa 1911.

RISHAD ASHURBEKOV
The long-awaited and only
baby boy, born in 1910 and
photographed in a way as to
not be mistaken for a girl. He
would later become a gifted
physician killed during WWII,
circa 1910.

Гавань. Баку.

The harbour.

Баку. Заводъ въ черномъ городѣ.

The factory by the black city.

Дворники.·

Janitors.

Street view with Alexander Nevsky Cathedral.

№ 57. Баку. — Bacou.
Древнія татарскія могилы. — Les anciens tombeaux tatares.

The ancient tombs of the Tatars.

№ 8 Реальное училище и Николаевская улица. Баку.
Ecole Réale et rue Nicolas. Bakou.

The Royal Academy and Nicholas Street.

The Horseman Magazine, Baku, 1908.

Cartoon "The Kardakyanskoy Road," from *The Horseman Magazine*, Issue 32, August 2, 1908.

Dubendi Terminal.

Баку. Александро-Невскій соборъ.

ALEXANDER NEVSKY CATHEDRAL

The largest Russian Orthodox church in the Caucasus, erected during 1888–98 and demolished by the Communists in the mid-1930s. The eighty-five-meter-high Cathedral was the highest construction in all of Baku. The church was built in the place of an old Muslim cemetery with even older, pre-Islamic graves discovered underneath. This unlucky placement of the church initially caused negative sentiments in the indigenous population. The church was designed by R. R. Marfeld, with the first brick laid by the penultimate Russian Emperor, Alexander III, hence the Cathedral's dedication to Saint Alexander. Construction of the church took nearly ten years and was completed by a young Polish civil engineer, Joseph Goslavski. The Azerbaijani population of the area had nicknamed the church Gyzylly Kilse (The Golden Church) for its shining golden domes.

The Destruction of the Alexander
Nevsky Cathedral
Baku, circa mid-1930s.

БАКУ Ханская мечеть.

Khan's Mosque.

The great Orthodox church, Baku.

Э. Л. Нобель среди рабочихъ въ Баку.

F. L. Nobel amongst workers in Baku.

Baku's "Inner City": History & Traditions

FARID ALAKBARLI

————
————

What Is Azerbaijan and Who Are the Azerbaijanians?

In the current territory of Azerbaijan, there live a people historically called the Azerbaijanians, or the Azeri Turks. Having resided in the area for centuries, they are today an independent nation with a distinct identity and culture. Genetically and culturally, they are most closely linked to the Oghuz Turks that occupy the Anatolian Peninsula.

The earliest nations to occupy this territory, in the first millennium BCE, were the Mannea, the Medes, and the Caucasian Albanians. Later, in medieval times, this area became the seat of empires belonging to the Seljuks, the Atabeks, the Akkoyunlu, the Karakoyunlu, the Safavids, the Afshars, and the Qajars.

Azerbaijan has always been a bridge between East and West, and between Asia and Europe. Azerbaijanis feel that their culture unites the mind of the West with the wisdom of the East, the logic of Europe with the soul of Asia. They have incorporated many of the ancient traditions of the Turkic, Caucasian, and Persian peoples that surround the country.

Officially, the Azerbaijanis adopted Islam between the seventh and eighth centuries of the Common Era. However, most of the population lead secular lives and have historically been tolerant of a plurality of ideas, beliefs, and religions. The division of state and religion has a strong basis. In 1918 Azerbaijan was proclaimed the first republic in the Muslim East. It possessed the first parliamentary democracy in the Orient and was the first democratic Turkic state.[1]

Ethnically, modern Azeris are descendants of the Oghuz Turks who mixed with various Caucasian and Persian tribes.[2] By the sixth century CE, the Oghuz Turkic Empire extended from China to the Black Sea. By the ninth century, they had taken over nearly the entire Middle East, first founding the Seljuk Empire in the eleventh century, and then the Ottoman Empire in the fourteenth century. Between the fourteenth and twentieth centuries, the Oghuz Turks of Azerbaijan established the Karakoyunlu, Akkoyunlu, Safavid, Avshar, and Qajar Empires, many of which at various times occupied all of Persia and parts of Central Asia and were key rivals of the Ottoman Empire.

The language of Azerbaijan is Azeri, which is closely related to the Turkish spoken in Turkey and the Turkmen spoken in Turkmenistan. This language group represents an extensive number of related dialects spoken widely throughout Asia and Eastern Europe, from Siberia to the Mediterranean, with nearly 160 million native speakers. Of these, some forty to fifty million are Azeri Turks, although only about nine million of these live in the Republic of Azerbaijan. The number of Azeri Turks who live in Iran is estimated to be between twenty-eight and thirty-five million (official Iranian sources do not break down information based on ethnic composition).

1. Baykara, *History of Struggle of Azerbaijan for Independence in Azerbaijan*, 231–51.
2. Sumbatzadeh, *Azerbaijanians–Ethnogenesis and Formation of the Nation*, 7.

Ties with Iran and Turkey

In their language and their identity, Azeris feel a close kinship with Turkey, in spite of the fact that the two nations were historically split by state borders and by differences in their interpretation of Islam. Turkey is overwhelmingly Sunni, while Azerbaijan is overwhelmingly Shia, like its neighbor Iran. During the Middle Ages, the Azeris, who were then under the rule of the Safavid Dynasty (1501-1736), led a drawn-out war against the Ottoman Empire. Today many in both Azerbaijan and Turkey refer to this time as the "war between two brothers." In 1918 the Turkish troops of General Nuru Pasha helped Azerbaijan to keep its independence. Even today, Turkey is the closest ally to Azerbaijan in the political arena. The former president of Azerbaijan, Heydar Aliyev, even referred to the two countries as "one nation, two states."[3]

Azerbaijanians also feel a close bond with neighboring Iran. For many centuries, Azerbaijan was included in vast empires that also encompassed Iran, Iraq, and much of central Asia. Today many Azeris live in the northwest provinces of Iran: East Azerbaijan, Ardabil, Zanjan, Hamedan, Qazvin, West Azerbaijan, and Markazi. There are also considerable populations in Tehran and Fars, and throughout other regions. Generally, these people refer to themselves as Turks or Azeri Turks. For several centuries, Persia was ruled by Turkic dynasties based in Azerbaijan, such as the Safavid Dynasty (1501-1722) in the ancient city of Ardabil. Shah Ismail I Safavid (1487-1524) penned verses in both Azeri and Persian, and his army, known as the Kizilbash (or "the Redheaded"), consisted completely of Turkic tribes from Azerbaijan, including the Bayat, the Avshar, the Shamlu, the Rumlu, the Karamanlu, the Zulkadar, and the Baharlu. Several famous Persian governors, such as Nadir Shah Afshar (1688-1747), as well as the shahs of the Qajar Dynasty (1725-1925) were not ethnic Persians but representatives of the Turkic tribes of Avshar and Qajar.

The effect of Persian culture and literature on Azerbaijan was significant. The poetry of Saadi, Hafiz, and Khayyam was always extremely popular. Muhammad Fuzuli (1494-1556), a Turkic poet who lived in Baghdad, wrote poems in Azeri, Persian, and Arabic. The musical genre *mugam* (*makam*) is characteristic of both Azerbaijan and Iran. The musical instruments of Azerbaijan (the *tar, zurna, kamancha, naghara* have close counterparts in Iran). There is a similarity in the two countries'

Lowering an oil rig.

3. "Heydar Aliyev and Turkism" (web publication).

cuisines as well. Like Iranians, Azeris favor pilafs, kebabs, and the same types of sweets. Therefore, we may conclude that contemporary Iranian culture includes a strong element of Turkic and Azeri influence.

The Rock Carvings of Prehistoric Baku

The area around Baku has been inhabited since prehistoric times. Abundant evidence of early human settlement has been found at the plain of Gobustan just south of Baku, between the southeastern slope of the Greater Caucasus Range and the Caspian Sea. Numerous petroglyphs dating from 10,000 BCE to the Middle Ages dot the region, making it one of the most important sites of ancient rock engravings in the world.

The rock drawings of Gobustan are incredibly diverse in terms of theme and content. Many drawings date as far back as the early Neolithic era, between the tenth and sixth millennia BCE. Among them one can find pictures of human beings, wild bulls, deer, Bezoar goats, lions, gazelles, horses, and wild asses, many of them close to life size. Other drawings represent labor, such as reaping, sacrifice, hunting, and battle scenes. One picture, for example, depicts a group of dancers in a circle with their arms thrown around each other's shoulders, perhaps a forerunner of the Yalli danced in Azerbaijan to this day.

A number of drawings from the early Neolithic period contain images of boats with armed and unarmed oarsmen, often depicting the sun on their bows. These ancient people held a belief that the sun, after declining in the west, was transported at night by boat so that it could begin its ascent in the east each morning. The many similarities between these petroglyphs—particularly that of the reed boat used to transport the sun—and those found in Norway attracted the attention of the famous Norwegian explorer Thor Heyerdahl. According to Heyerdahl, these drawings "testify to the fact that boats were of extreme importance to early man, as they provided security and transportation millennia before there were roads cut into the wilderness."[4] Based on the archaeological findings and on the content of the petroglyphs, Heyerdahl theorized that it was likely that the ancestors of Scandinavians, including Norwegians such as himself, came from the region known as Azerbaijan.

Alongside these ancient pictorial records, one of the rocks of Gobustan bears a Latin inscription dating between 84 and 96 CE. It describes the visit of a centurion from the Roman Twelfth Legion, known as the Fulminata ("Lightning"), which passed through Gobustan in the first century CE during the reign of the emperor Domitian. The inscription was made by the Roman legioneer Lucius Julius Maximus and reads, "Under emperor Domitian, Caesar, Augustus Germanicus, Lucius Julius Maximus, Legio XII Fulminatat." This was the same Twelfth Legion

---

4. Heyerdahl, "Challenging Euro-Centric Theories of Migration," 60.

that fought at the Battle of Pharsalus (48 BCE) when Caesar defeated Pompey. The inscriptions attest to the fact that the Twelfth Legion was also in the Caucasus region, including the area around Baku, in the first century.[5]

To preserve the rich heritage of its ancient culture, as well as the natural remnants of the past, in 1966 Gobustan was designated a protected national heritage site, with an area of 4,400 hectares (almost eleven thousand acres). The aim of the open-area museum is to preserve the Gobustan site while keeping it accessible to the public. Today thousands of visitors from all over the world who are interested in the history of early civilizations visit the petroglyphs of Gobustan each year.

Christianity in Baku

The spread of Christianity in Azerbaijan is associated with the kingdom of Caucasian Albania, which occupied nearly all of the territory of present-day Azerbaijan between the fourth century and eighth century CE. The polytheistic religion of Albania was centered on the worship of three divinities whom the Roman histories interpreted as Sol, Zeus, and Luna. The Turkic tribes of Caucasian Albania—such as the Huns, the Khazars, the Bulgars, and the Sabirs—worshipped Tengri, the Turkic God of the Blue Sky.

In some parts of Caucasian Albania, including Baku, there were Zoroastrians derived from ancient Persia. Because Baku was rich in oil and gas resources, it attracted Zoroastrians who worshipped natural phenomena such as the eternal fires and burning oil fields around Baku. Zoroastrianism became the strongest force against Christianity in the Caucasus.

Christianity arrived in Caucasian Albania during the first centuries after Christ, as the first waves of missionaries began to arrive from Syria and Jerusalem. Saint Bartholomew, one of Christ's twelve apostles, is perhaps the best-known preacher of the gospel ever to set foot in the territory of present-day Azerbaijan. He traveled from India, following the many caravan routes of pilgrims heading toward fire country, as Caucasian Albania was the center of Zoroastrianism. Tradition holds that Bartholomew was martyred by pagan priests who were infuriated by the success of his sermons.

One legend tells that Saint Bartholomew was murdered in the Temple of Arta in Baku at the order of King Astiag. Orthodox Christians still hold that the Maiden Tower in Baku is the same Temple of Arta where Saint Bartholomew was slaughtered by outraged Zoroastrians. After the nineteenth-century conquest of Baku by the Russians, Christians erected a small church dedicated to Saint Bartholomew right next to the Maiden Tower. The church was destroyed during the Stalinist era in the 1930s, at a time when religion was systematically persecuted under the Union of Soviet Socialist Republics (USSR) policies.

5. Ashurbeyli, *History of Baku City . . .*, 31.

Древнее Мусульманское кладбище. БАКУ.
Cimetière ancienne de Muselman. BAKOU.

Ancient Muslim cemetery.

Saint Eliseus was the second well-known Christian missionary to the land of present-day Azerbaijan. Eliseus made his way through much of Caucasian Albania and visited the ancient village of Kish near the town of Sheki, where he had a church built that still stands to this day and remains a point of pilgrimage for many.[6]

The Caucasian Albanian Church experienced hardship throughout much of its long existence, and adhered to the Eastern Synod during the Great Schism. In the year 498 (488 according to some sources), in the settlement Aluen or Aghuen (presently known as the Agdam region of Azerbaijan), an Albanian church council convened to adopt laws to strengthen the position of Christianity in Caucasian Albania.

Members of the church took part in further missionary efforts in the Caucasus and in the Pontic-Caspian steppe. During the sixth and seventh centuries, the Bible was translated into the Turkic Hun language. In 682 the patriarch of the Albanian Church based in Israel led an unsuccessful delegation to convert Alp Iluetuer, the

6. Sumbatzadeh, *Azerbaijanians–Ethnogenesis and Formation of the Nation,* 60.

№ 2 Лютеранская церковь. Баку.
L'Eglise Luthérienne. Bakou.

THE LUTHERAN CHURCH IN BAKU
Built in 1895–98, designed by
A. Eichler.

ruler of the North Caucasian Huns, to Christianity. This same church maintained a number of monasteries in the Holy Land.

The Albanian Church suffered a great deal under the sweeping influence of Islam, although it continued to exist right up until 1836, when the Russian Empire that had recently gained control of Azerbaijan abruptly put an end to its existence.

Zoroastrianism in Baku

Prior to the introduction of Islam in the region of Azerbaijan during the seventh century, the people who lived in the area were Zoroastrians who worshipped fire. The Absheron Peninsula around Baku became a spiritual hub for Zoroastrianism due to a curious natural phenomenon. So much oil is buried deep inside the ground there that the gas seeps out through fissures in the earth's surface and periodically catches fire. These sites in Surakhani and in other areas around Baku were considered sacred, and fire-worshipping temples were built there. In medieval times, Zoroastrians believed that Azerbaijan was the native land of the Prophet Zarathustra (Zoroaster), who, according to legend, was born in the city of Urmiyya, today the capital of the West Azerbaijan province in Iran.

To this day, a gas torch burns atop Baku's famous Maiden Tower. Some scholars believe that the Maiden Tower was originally used for defensive purposes. Others

A leaf from "The Picturesque Caucasus. Drawn from nature by Prince Gregory Gagarin," Paris, 1847.

Shiite Ceremony of Shakhsey-Vakhsey, Baku, 1888.

Praying Tatar in Baku, 1888.

suggest that it was used as a Zoroastrian temple as far back as 2,500 years ago. Archaeological excavations have revealed an altar located near the base of the Maiden Tower. The altar's stone basin contained traces of oil and fire, leading many to believe that the basin was kept filled with oil in order to keep an eternal fire burning. Professor Davud Akhundov has asserted that during the first millennium BC there was a Temple of Fire in the Water located on the Caspian Sea coast directly in front of the Maiden Tower.[7]

Baku's oil continued to be used as a source of Holy Fire even during the Middle Ages, after most Azerbaijanis had converted to Islam. In the eighteenth century, the burning oil of the Absheron Peninsula attracted fire worshippers from India who built a Temple of Fire (Atashgah) in the Surakhani village near Baku. These Zoroastrians and followers of Shiva worshipped the eternal, sacred fire that was nourished by the oil and gas burning inside the temple. As for the city of Baku, archaeological evidence suggests that there was a large settlement around the Maiden Tower dating from at least the first centuries of the Common Era.

Conversion to Islam

A new cultural era began following the invasion of Azerbaijan by the Arabs and the subsequent spread of Islam. The conquest of Azerbaijan by the Arabs began in 643 with brilliantly coordinated multipronged attacks by Caliph Umar that paralyzed what little remained of the Sassanid Empire. Hudeifa ibn Al Yaman was appointed the commander in charge of conquering Azerbaijan. Hudeifa marched from Rayy to Zanjan, at which point he was called back by Caliph Umar. Bukair ibn Abdullah and Utba ibn Farquad succeeded him and were sent to carry out a two-pronged attack. A pact was drawn according to which Azerbaijan surrendered to Caliph Umar on the standard terms of paying an annual *jizya*, a tax on non-Muslims. From this point onward, Azerbaijan began the gradual process of converting to Islam, a process that took centuries to complete. Even as late as the tenth century, many Christians and Zoroastrians lived in Azerbaijan.

Once Islam was introduced, several branches of the sciences began to grow by leaps and bounds, particularly in the field of medicine. Overall, the cultural effects of Islam were incredibly substantial. The great empire forged by the Arabs, called the caliphate, rapidly spread and brought together many diverse cultures of the Islamic world. Since that time, the Azeri, Turkish, Persian, Indian, Greek, Arabic, and other various cultures have deeply influenced one another. The great range of scientific traditions located within the boundaries of this common empire led to an unprecedented era of rich exchange in all areas of daily life, science, and culture.

7. Akhundov, *Architecture of Ancient and Medieval Azerbaijan*, 98–112.

Baku as the Capital of Azerbaijan

Between the twelfth century and the year 1538, Baku served as the capital of the Shirvanshah state after Shamakhi, a city an hour-and-a-half drive north of Baku, sustained a major earthquake. Once the Shirvanshah state (799–1538) was taken over by the Safavid Dynasty from the south in the year 1538, Baku was relegated to being a city in the Shirvan Province of the Safavid state.[8]

Between 1747 and 1806, Baku again became a capital of a khanate that included thirty-nine surrounding villages. This independent principality, sometimes called Badkube (meaning "wind-beaten" or "city of winds") even coined its own money. In 1806 Baku was subsumed by the Russian Empire until May 28, 1918.

The third time Baku was established as a capital city was in 1918, after the collapse of the Russian Empire and the proclamation of the Democratic Republic of Azerbaijan. In 1920 Baku remained the capital of the Azerbaijan Soviet Socialist Republic, officially becoming a part of the Union of Soviet Socialist Republics in 1922. After 1991 the Republic of Azerbaijan declared independence, and Baku continued to function as the capital.

Oil well, Balakhan, 1888.

Early Oil Explorations in Baku

Azerbaijan has long been known for its rich oil resources. The earliest exploration of onshore oil fields dates back to at least the seventh century BCE, during the age of the Median kingdom in what is now referred to as Southern Azerbaijan in Iran. The Median province that bordered Assyria became the first place in the world to extract oil from wells. Starting in the fifth century BCE, oil was drawn from shallow wells in leather buckets.

Oil played an important role in the everyday lives of the Medians, the Caspians, and other ancient tribes of Azerbaijan. It was used as fuel to fill lamps of clay and metal. Oil also made a useful weapon; Median warriors would apply oil to the tips of their arrows, javelins, and spears. Once lit, the projectiles could be hurled or catapulted into enemy encampments and onto ships. The ancient Greeks referred to this ancient technique of flame throwing as "Median oil."

During the Middle Ages, oil began to be extracted on a somewhat larger scale, particularly from the Absheron Peninsula. Between the tenth and thirteenth centuries, "light crude oil" was drawn from the Balakhani village, and "heavy crude oil" from Surakhani.

As for distillation, Azerbaijanians have been familiar with the practice since the first centuries of the Common Era. In the thirteenth century, geographer Ibn Bekran wrote that oil was distilled in Baku to minimize its bad smell and to make it more acceptable for medicinal applications. Around this same time, Marco Polo recorded that high-grade Baku oil was commonly used for illuminating houses and

Village of Balakhan near Baku, 1888.

8. Ashurbeyli, *The State of Shirvanshahs,* 4–22.

Azeri women.

View of the Old City and the Juma Mosque.

Дѣвичья Башня. Баку.

The Qiz Qalasi (Maiden Tower).

A street in the fortress.

City garden.

Городской Садъ.   Баку.

The city garden.

74 Leaves from the album, "Scenes, Landscapes, Customs and Costumes of the Caucasus. Drawn from nature by Prince Gregory Gagarin," Paris, 1847.

treating skin diseases. The Azerbaijani geographer Abd ar-Rashid Bakuvi, writing around the turn of the fifteenth century, noted that up to two hundred camel bales of oil were exported from Baku every day. A single "camel bale" is the equivalent of roughly three hundred kilograms of oil, so this would have meant a regular supply of sixty thousand kilograms of oil leaving Baku every day.

According to Hamdullah Gazvini, writing in the fourteenth century, workers used to fill oil wells with water, forcing the oil to rise to the surface, at which point it was collected with the aid of leather bags made from the skin of Caspian seals. As late as 1669, the scholar Muhammad Mu'min noted that such leather bags were still in common use for the storage and transport of oil.

In 1572 British merchant Jeffrey Decket visited Baku and recorded his observations of the city. According to his account, large amounts of oil had seeped to the earth's surface. Many people traveled to the city to obtain this oil, some from considerable distances. Decket wrote that a type of black oil, called "naft," was used throughout the country to illuminate homes. This oil was transported to faraway lands on the backs of mules or donkeys in caravans consisting of up to five hundred animals. In the immediate vicinity of Baku, Decket noted a white, exceedingly precious kind of oil, writing that it was "similar to our petroleum (the mountainous oil)."[9]

9. Hakluyt, *The Principal Navigations,* 347.

In 1601 Persian historian Amin Ahmad ar-Razi wrote that there were five hundred oil wells in the vicinity of Baku from which oil was extracted on a daily basis. Katib Chelebi, a Turkish historian of the same period, quotes these same figures. Lerch, the seventeenth-century German traveler, writes that there were three to four hundred oil wells on the Absheron Peninsula, and, furthermore, that a single well in Balakhani village produced three thousand kilograms of oil on a daily basis.

German scholar and secretary of the Swedish embassy Engelbert Kaempfer (1651–1716) visited Baku in 1683 and recorded in his diary that oil wells were routinely up to twenty-seven meters deep, with walls covered in limestone or wood. He wrote that Surakhani, a village not far from Baku, possessed wells that could produce between 2,700 and 3,000 kilograms a day, filling eighty carriages bearing eight oil bags apiece. During this period, Baku oil was already being exported to Russia and other countries in Eastern Europe.[10]

Oil extraction led to the pollution of the environment as far back as the Middle Ages, although this gave cause for concern only in recent times. Azerbaijani author Muhammad Yusif Shirvani wrote in his "Tibbname" (Book of medicine) in 1712 that both the soil and water of the area had become contaminated as a result of oil and sulfur extraction.

10. Kaempfer, *Amoenitatum exoticarum*, 278–279.

Баку. Храмъ Огнепоклонниковъ.

Sourakhany, the temple of fire worship.

According to British missionary Father Willot, who visited Azerbaijan in 1689, the annual income that the Safavid shahs derived from Baku oil was 7,000 *tumans*, or 420,000 French livres.[11]

Oil as Medicine

Oil and oil-based products were widely used for medicinal purposes during the Middle Ages, according to sources on medical and pharmaceutical practices that are currently held at Baku's Institute of Manuscripts. Mineral oil was used in ointments that were applied externally against such conditions as neurological disorders, listlessness, paralysis, and seizures. Oil was also used to treat chest pains, coughing, asthma, and rheumatism.

In *Jam-al-Baghdadi* (Baghdad collection), written in 1311, Azerbaijani author Yusif Khoyi addresses the use of oil and bitumen in medicine, stating that

11. *Voyages*, 100.

ointments made from oil were applied to the skin to treat tumors, eyedrops were made to heal cataracts, and eardrops to treat earaches.

In his 1669 *Tukhfat al-mu'minin* (Gift of true believers), Muhammad Mu'min recommended the use of oil-based remedies for asthma, chronic coughs, colic, dyspepsia, and intestinal parasites. Along those same lines, seventeenth-century Azerbaijani Hasan bin Riza Shirvani described the curative effects of "white oil" (kerosene), "blue oil" (weakly distilled oil), "black oil" (unrefined oil), and bitumen.

Oil was used for veterinary purposes as well. Abdurrashid Bakuvi, a fifteenth-century scientist whose father was from Baku, wrote of oil's antiseptic properties. According to Bakuvi, residents of Baku and Absheron treated the coats of their camels with oil to protect them from mange.

In modern Azerbaijan, oil is still used medicinally, particularly *naftalan,* a unique type of oil found only in the north-central part of the country, where a therapeutic spa has been built. Several spas in and around Baku incorporate oil into their healing regimens.

Alexandre Dumas and the Land of Fire

In 1858 the great French novelist Alexandre Dumas (1802–1870) visited the Caucasus. On his nine-month journey through the region, one of the places that captured his imagination most was Atashgah, the fire temple located on the outskirts of Baku. Dumas recorded his impressions in his *Travels in the Caucasus,* which was published the following year in Paris. Dumas challenged his fellow Frenchmen not to delay in visiting this incredible site. How correct he was. Today the Atashgah compound has been converted into a museum and is no longer the living monument that Dumas so richly described. The fire worshippers are long gone, and the flames no longer burn spontaneously in the domed cupola. Instead, the eternal flame is fed from gas channeled in through pipes underground. Here is the scene as Dumas witnessed it approximately 150 years ago:

> After breakfast we took our seats in the phaeton that was waiting for us at the front door and headed out to the famous Atashgah. Baku's Atashgah is known throughout the entire world, that is, with the exception of the French, who rarely travel. This site that is on fire both day and night is situated twenty-six kilometers distant from Baku. The eternal flames emanate from the black and crude oil beneath the ground.
>
> It took us two hours to arrive at Atashgah. During the first part of our journey we traveled along the seashore. At Atashgah we climbed to the top of a hill, from where we could view all of Atashgah with its fires. Just imagine an area of 4.5 square kilometers!
>
> Great tongues of flame soared in the air from the hundreds of tiny round fissures in the ground. The wind would scatter the flames, curve them and then

straighten them, spreading them along the ground and then lifting them up to the heavens again. It was impossible for the wind to extinguish them.

There was a big quadrangular building that was also lit by a fire. Reflections of the flames danced on the walls of the building, making it seem as if the building itself was moving.

There was a whitewashed temple, surrounded by little ovens, again filled with tongues of flame. The gas burned with such a loud noise that each of these little ovens sounded like a big furnace. On the roof, great tongues of flame were emitted from each of the four corners of the big cupola. But these flames were weaker than the fire nearby the eastern entrance of the temple.

We approached the compound through a single gate situated in the east. Then a spectacular and very beautiful view opened up before our very eyes. It is said that this place is usually only illuminated like this on holidays. It turned out that M. Pigulevski [the Russian authority in Baku] had notified the people at Atashgah about our arrival. These fire worshippers, who have experienced

A street in the fortress.

Баку. (Bacou).
Улица въ крѣпости. (Une rue de la forteresse).

repression for more than two thousand years, obeyed his order and prepared everything to the best of their ability.

My compatriots who would like to see these fire worshippers had better hurry. The only worshippers left are an old man and two others around thirty to thirty-five years old. One of the young men had just arrived from India only six months earlier. That is, before him there were only two worshippers left at Atashgah.

We entered through a door that was completely enveloped by flames. In the middle of a big quadrangular court, there was a domed building with an altar in it. In the middle of the altar, an eternal flame was burning. The gas flames were also emitted in all four corners of the dome. It was necessary to climb five or six stairs to approach the altar.

Approximately twenty cells were situated along the external wall that opened up to the courtyard. These cells were built for disciples who were preparing themselves to become Zoroastrians. In one cell, there was a niche for displaying two idols.

One of the worshippers robed himself in a priest's vesture. Another, who was completely naked, put on something like a shirt, and the worship rituals commenced.

During the ceremony, the priest sang, altering his voice in a most unusual manner. He also performed a song that consisted of four or five chromatic notes ranging between "sol" and "mi," and in which the name of Brahma was frequently invoked. At times the priest prostrated himself facedown on the ground. Another of the fire worshippers beat upon the porcelain plates he held in his hands, producing a high and ringing noise. After the worship ceremony had ended, the priest presented to each of us a bit of sugar candy. In turn, each of us gave him one ruble.

Dumas ended his account by saying, "We visited the Mount Vesuvius of Baku. The Atashgah is greater than the Mount Vesuvius volcano of Naples because it burns eternally. Then we returned to Baku."[12]

Inner City, Outer City

Baku's Icheri Sheher, which literally means "inner city" but is often referred to by foreigners as the "old city," is a unique architectural preserve that differs considerably from the other ancient places of Azerbaijan. Icheri Sheher (pronounced *ee-char-EE sha-HAR*) boasts numerous architectural monuments, including the Maiden Tower and Shirvanshah Palace, which is currently undergoing renovation. Moreover, the medieval Inner City has historically had a distinct culture and set

12. Dumas, *Caucasus*, 189–91.

of traditions, many of which are starting to be lost and forgotten. Reconstructing the ethnographic features of the community that once lived behind Icheri Sheher's fortified walls is a formidable task. Most of today's Azerbaijanis know almost nothing of the history or traditions that once characterized the Inner City. As the older generations pass on, fewer and fewer know firsthand of Icheri Sheher's way of life, folk art, holidays, oral history, and anecdotes.

For most of Baku's history, the entire town was located within the fortress walls that held a population of around seven thousand. After the Russians had occupied the city in 1806, and especially after the first oil boom that took place between 1850 and 1920, Baku grew rapidly beyond its fortified walls. During these years the expressions *icheri sheher* and *bayir sheher* (Outer City) first came into common usage.

Huseingulu Sarabski (1879-1945), the famous Azeri actor and author of the book *Old Baku* wrote, "Baku is divided into two sections: Icheri Sheher and Bayir Sheher. The Inner City was the main part. Those who lived in the Inner City were considered natives of Baku. They were in close proximity to everything: the bazaar, craftsmen's workshops, and mosques. There was even a church there, as well as a military barracks built during the Russian occupation." Residents who lived inside the walls considered themselves superior to those on the outside, often referring to them as "those barefooted people of the Outer City."[13]

The Inner City is composed of many small neighborhoods demarcated by winding lanes and narrow streets. Originally, each section or block was named for the closest mosque: Juma Mosque Block, Shal Mosque Block, Mohammadyar Mosque Block, Haji Gayib Mosque Block, Sinigalla Mosque Block, Gasimbey Mosque Block, and so on. Some sections of the Inner City and their mosques were named after the clans and nationalities that lived there. For instance, Gilaklar was the place where merchants from Gilan resided. Lezgilar was the street where Dagestani armorers and gunsmiths lived. Many of the Inner City's inhabitants were craftsmen, merchants, or seamen. Several of the Inner City's blocks derived their names from certain professions, such as Hamamchilar (bathhouse owners), Bazarlar (cloth traders), and Hakkakchilar (stone engravers).

When tallied up in 1806, the Inner City boasted 707 workshops and ateliers, even though the total population was only seven thousand. Each merchant or craftsman had his own store. Their customers were visitors from other lands who had come to trade in Baku. Ships leaving Baku carried goods to Iran, central Asia, and Russia.

13. Sarabski, *Old Baku,* 121.

№ 120. Баку. — Bacou.
Дѣвичья башня (Кизъ-Кали).
Tour de la Jeune-Fille (Kiskalé).

The Maiden Tower (The Qiz Qalasi).

Centuries-Old Monuments

The Inner City's surviving ancient monuments include the Maiden Tower, the Sinig Gala Minaret or Mosque of Muhammad (1078/79 CE), the fortress walls and towers (eleventh and twelfth centuries), and Shirvanshah Palace (fifteenth and sixteenth centuries). In addition, the Inner City once boasted twenty-eight mosques, nine caravanserai, several bathhouses, *ovdans* (potable water reservoirs), and a bazaar. Merchants from central Asia tended to stay in the fifteenth-century Bukhari caravanserai, while Indian traders preferred the fourteenth-century Multani caravanserai.

Baku's residents shared a perennial fondness for bathhouses. Aside from a bath, one could also get a massage, enjoy refreshments such as cool *sharbat* (fruit drinks) or hot tea, have a snack, or partake of a hookah. Several of Baku's old bathhouses are still standing, including the large fifteenth-century Haji Gayib bathhouse behind the Maiden Tower, and the seventeenth-century Gasimbey bathhouse located near the British Council Cultural Department.

While Baku's medieval bazaar no longer exists, its columns and archways are still in evidence next to the Maiden Tower. In the early twentieth century, the bazaar was enlarged to extend from the Multani and Bukhari caravanserais to the fourteenth-century Juma Mosque.

Maiden Tower

The Maiden Tower is one of Baku's more prominent and striking monuments. From the air, the uniquely shaped structure resembles a giant comma, with its cylindrical eight-story stone tower attached to a large stone ledge.

The origins of the tower remain a mystery to this day. Historians continue to debate even the most basic assumptions, questioning when it was built and what purpose its strange design might have served.

When Soviet archaeologists and historians researched the Maiden Tower, they misidentified it as a military fortress built in the twelfth century by the architect Masud ibn Davud, whose name was found on a stone inserted into one of the walls. Later, historian Sara Ashurbeyli proved that the stone was merely a fragment of a tombstone used to repair the tower.

Only after Azerbaijan gained independence did architectural historian Shamil Fatullayev publish his *Architectural Encyclopedia of Baku*, in which the tower is dated to the pre-Islamic period thirteen hundred years ago.

Professor Davud Akhundov developed yet another striking theory. He believes that the tower was never used for military purposes but rather served as an ancient Zoroastrian fire-worshiping temple. Akhundov writes in his book *The Architecture of Ancient and Early Medieval Azerbaijan*, "At the beginning of the first millennium BCE, there was an eight-storied temple (Maiden Tower) devoted to seven gods, grandiose for those days: there were seven sacred levels, wall-recessed altars with seven-colored fires burning in honor of the Pantheon of Gods of Ahura Mazda or Mithra."[14]

While no one knows for sure why the Maiden Tower was built, we do know for certain that it was not built in the twelfth century, as previously thought, but rather many centuries earlier.

Shirvanshah's Palace

The medieval Shirvanshah's Palace remains an important symbol for Azerbaijanis, reminding them of Azerbaijan's history as an independent state. During Soviet times, several biased academics attempted to prove that Azerbaijan had never functioned independently but rather was ruled by other nations such as Russia and Persia up until 1918. Unfortunately, a few Azerbaijanis and foreigners continue to subscribe to this notion to this day. However, the preponderance of historical

14. Akhundov, *Architecture*, 287.

evidence suggests that Shirvan (Northern Azerbaijan), including the palace, functioned as an independent state for nearly seven hundred years, between the ninth and sixteenth centuries.

The Shirvanshah's Palace that dominates Old Baku was erected between the fifteenth and sixteenth centuries. It is one of the few remaining large palaces from this era not destroyed by marauders or invaders in later years. The two-story main building of the palace complex once contained an elaborate gold-plated throne. In front of this building stands the mausoleum of the fifteenth-century scholar Seyid Yahya Bakuvi. An adjacent building called the Divankhana (Court of Law) boasts portals adorned with intricate stone carvings. The lower yard of the complex contains the burial vault of the Shirvan shahs as well as a mosque and the remains of an ancient bathhouse.

Shirvanshah's Palace did not function as a working palace for long. In 1500 CE, Baku was captured by Shah Ismayil Safavi of the city of Ardabil in Southern Azerbaijan (now Iran). He completely conquered the existing Shirvan state, killing its leaders and burning many of its buildings.

In Soviet times, Shirvanshah's Palace was open to the public as a museum. Today the museum is closed and the palace has undergone extensive renovation. Its future as a public institution is uncertain.

European Architectural Styles

After the Russian government took control of Baku in the early nineteenth century, the traditional look of the Inner City began to change. Many extraordinary buildings of the European type were constructed during the nineteenth century and early twentieth centuries, incorporating neo-baroque and Gothic styles.

One such building, formerly known as the Chain House, is home to Baku's Institute of Ethnography today. This building's roof at one time boasted three classical statues of women and two amphoras, in imitation of ancient Greece. The pedestals of the sculptures were joined with a double iron chain, eventually giving rise to the name Zanjirli Ev or Chain House. All of the sculptures were removed during the Soviet period, and today only the oldest of residents still refers to it as the Chain House. Recently, however, the central statue of the building's façade has been carefully reconstructed.

As you enter the Inner City through the double gates there is, to the left of the Institute of Ethnography, a three-story early modern dwelling built in 1903 by the sea captain Abdul-Manaf Alakbarzadeh ("Alekperov" in Russian spelling). Alakbarzadeh resided on the third floor, and his brother Museyib, also a sea captain, resided on the second floor. Their other brother, Mammad Sadikh, a banker, lived on the first floor. Together they owned the smaller adjoining building, which today is covered with grapevines, and leased it out to various shopkeepers.

Kalinin, portrait of Paul Dmitrievich Tsitsianov, 1820–30, lithograph.

Caravanserai at Titsianov Square, Baku, 1887.

Inner City businessman Zeynalabdin Taghiyev (1837–1915) built a lovely Baroque-style building just to the right of the Chain House. Unfortunately, that building was torn down in 1970 and replaced by a Soviet concrete block structure that today is known as the Encyclopedia Building.

The Double Gates and General Tsitsianov

Huseyngulu Sarabski, in his book *Old Baku,* provides an interesting and concise history of the Baku fortress gates, which were built between the twelfth and nineteenth centuries. In 1930 Sarabski wrote, "Recently the Inner City has acquired a fifth gate, although in the past there were only four. The most famous of these entrances is the Double Fortress Gate (Gosha Gala), at times referred to as the Shamakhi Gate."[15] According to my elderly relatives, Gosha Gala used to consist of only one entrance, not the two that exist today that allow traffic to enter and exit through separate doorways.

Apparently, the Russian General Pavel Tsitsianov was keen to capture the Old City through these particular gates. In 1806 the Russian navy landed its troops on the shores of Baku Bay. General Tsitsianov sought permission from Khan Huseingulu for a garrison of Russian soldiers to enter the city. At first the khan agreed and even went out to greet Tsitsianov in front of the double gates. But, while the negotiations were being carried out, the khan's cousin Ibrahim suddenly shot Tsitsianov.

Tsitsianov's soldiers fled, but the Khan's guard tracked them down and killed many of them. Then Baku's artillery opened fire on the Tsar's ships, which were attempting to make a hasty retreat to Sara Island, just off the coast. The khan beheaded Tsitsianov and sent the head to Fathali Shah in Persia as a gift. As Russia was at war with Persia, Huseingulu Khan was hoping to engage the Persian shah's assistance in combating the tsar's forces.

However, Fathali Shah's assistance was not forthcoming. Seven months later, on September 18, 1806, the Russians returned, this time easily capturing the whole of Baku. With only five hundred soldiers and seventy cannons, Huseingulu Khan could not withstand the superior Russian forces under Bulgakov. Huseingulu fled to Ardabil in Southern Azerbaijan.

In 1846 the Russians erected a monument in memory of Tsitsianov, placing it directly in front of the Double Fortress Gates, where he had been murdered. Following the Bolshevik Revolution in 1920, this monument was dismantled and destroyed, as it honored the tsar's army. This period of the history of Baku

15. Sarabski, *Old Baku,* 120.

is described in the book *Gullistani-Iram* (Garden of paradise) by the renowned scholar Abbasgulu Agha Bakikhanov (1794-1847), himself a descendant of Baku's last khan.

Gates and Trade

Huseyngulu Sarabski's *Old Baku* provides interesting information about another famous gate, Taghiyev Gate, located near what is now the Academy of Science Presidium. Sarabski writes, "Another gate is situated close to the Double Fortress Gates, near the Sabir Square."[16] This gate is not medieval and was built much later, in 1877, by the Baku merchant and landowner Haji Zeynalabdin Taghiyev (a namesake of the famous millionaire). Haji Zeynalabdin's nickname, Gatir, relates to the gate. Haji Zeynalabdin owned various shops just outside the fortress walls, where Sabir Garden and Husi Hajiyev Street are today. However, these shops were impossible to rent, as they were considered too far for customers to travel on foot from the Inner City's bazaar. Eventually, Haji Zeynalabdin came up with the idea of opening a section of the citadel wall and erecting a new gate there.

Once people from the Inner City were able to pass through the new gate, business at the shops began to flourish, which is how Haji got the nickname Gatir (Mule), a reference to his quick wit, resourcefulness, and stubbornness.

According to newspaper accounts, a heated battle took place in front of Taghiyev Gate in 1918, when Armenians attempted to capture the Inner City. Gatir Haji Zeynalabdin's son, Mammad Hanifa (1875-1920), nicknamed Gochu (Brave), actively participated in defending troops staving off an Armenian takeover. Murat Baykal in his book *Oil King from Baku* writes: "He, along with his friends and relatives blocked all entrances and exits of the Old City, and day and night were skirmishes with the Armenians, not allowing them to penetrate the fortress."[17]

A third gate opened into a courtyard of the former Industrial College, now the Azerbaijan State Economic University. Wheat and coal from the Absheron village of Navahi and from various mountain villages were brought to this gate by cart

The fortress entrance.

16. Ibid.
17. Baykal, *Oil King*, 29.

and camel. A fourth gate was situated behind Baku's city hall. The fifth gate opened from the governor's garden near the present-day Philharmonic Hall.

Baku Clans

The native Inner City dwellers historically belonged to several different clans, several of which had incredibly amusing nicknames. For example, some of the more influential clans were named: Agshalvarlilar (Those who wear white trousers), Toyugyeyanlar (Chicken eaters), Toyugyeymayanlar (Those who do not eat chicken), and Bozbashlilar (Gray- or bald-headed). Each clan made disparaging jokes and puns about the names of the others; for example, *bozbash* also refers to a much-loved Azerbaijani soup with meatballs, chickpeas, and sour plums. Thus, a corpulent member of the Bozbashlilar clan might jokingly be referred to as "the meatball from Bozbash." A diminutive member of the clan might be called "the chickpea from Bozbash." These days, the tradition of dividing residents into clans has completely stopped. Many young people cannot even name the clan to which their grandparents belonged.

Nicknames

When we read about the past inhabitants of the Old City, it seems as if almost everyone had a humorous nickname. For example, at one time there were five men living there by the name of Haji Zeynalabdin and each went by a different nickname. Residents referred to them as Malakesh (Plasterer), Gatir (Mule), Spasibo ("Thank you" in Russian), Nokar (Servant), and Pendiryemeyen (Cheese hater).

The millionaire philanthropist Haji Zeynalabdin Taghiyev got his nickname Plasterer after having spent his youth working as a mason. As the story went, one day Taghiyev discovered a clay jar filled with gold coins plastered into the walls of one of the homes he was working on. He sold the coins and purchased land that, luckily for him, proved to have a huge oil gusher. (Taghiyev himself consistently denied this tale.)

The Haji Zeynalabdin Taghiyev nicknamed Gatir (Mule) earned this title following his success and persistence in building Taghiyev Gate in the old citadel wall. Mules are believed to be so intelligent that they can literally find water in a desert. A person perceived to make money from nothing is often called *gatir*.

Writer Manaf Suleymanov recounts an amusing anecdote about Gatir Haji Zeynalabdin. Haji had a merchant friend who was having trouble selling his large supply of cookies. Haji took a box of the biscuits and hid his expensive ring inside the box (another version of this story has it that the object was a five-ruble coin). Then Haji went to the café at the Tabriz Hotel, opened the box, and began munching on the cookies. Several moments later, he exclaimed, "Look what I've found inside this box!" People rushed to buy the remaining boxes of cookies, and Haji's friend enjoyed a huge profit.

Марінинская Женская Гимназія.
Lycée pour filles de Marie.

Баку.
Bakou.

The Marie School for Girls.

87

The third Haji Zeynalabdin was called Spasibo (Thank you). Apparently, as recounted by author Manaf Suleymanov, he was determined to win a title, post, or medal when Tsar Alexander III visited Baku. Prior to the Tsar's arrival, Zeynalabdin repaired the Russian military barracks at his own expense. When the Tsar visited the barracks and met Zeynalabdin, he announced, *"Spasibo, Zeynalabdin!"* then abruptly turned and left, bestowing neither medal nor title. Zeynalabdin had spent enormous sums of money and received only a *"Spasibo"* in return. From then on, the residents of Icheri Sheher nicknamed Haji as Spasibo.

Elderly residents of the Inner City recall yet another Haji Zeynalabdin who had once been a servant of the wealthy oil baron Haji Zeynalabdin. Gradually, this servant established his own business and became enormously wealthy in his own right. But despite his wealth and status, people of the Inner City referred to him as Nokar (Servant) for the rest of his life.

Education

Historical records indicate that a *madrasa* (a religious secondary school) was set up in the Old City sometime during the eleventh century. It was there that the famous philosopher Baba Kuhi Bakuvi (933-1074) taught science. Four hundred years later another distinguished scholar, Seyid Yahya Bakuvi, founded a Sufi school in Shirvanshah's Palace that later became the renowned order of the Halvatiya. However, when the Shirvanshah state collapsed in 1538 and Baku lost its status as a capital, these important schools were shut down and the cultural life of the city began to gradually diminish. The tiny Baku khanate founded in 1744 could not replicate the sophisticated cultural environment of the earlier era.

When the Russians descended on Baku in 1806 there were a total of twelve primary and secondary religious schools in the Inner City. According to Sarabski, only three remained by the early 1900s and the quality of education had deteriorated. Most native residents referred to these schools as Mollakhana (Mullah's home). Education at the Mollakhanas was based solely on rote memorization. When students failed to correctly pronounce their Arabic vocabulary, they were beaten with a stick called a *chubug* until they mastered the pronunciation. Likewise, during calligraphy lessons teachers would often hit the children's fingers when they made mistakes. When parents took their sons to the Mollakhana, they would often repeat the proverb, "The flesh is yours, but the bones are mine!" Capital punishment of all kinds existed at both the Mollakhanas and the Russian schools. Prior to the advent of the Russian education system, the only avenue for attaining a basic education was through the Mollakhana, where young boys could study the Arabic alphabet, calligraphy, grammar, and arithmetic. Additionally, they would memorize the entire Koran and occasionally read verses by Saadi and Hafiz in Farsi. Through *Tarikhi-Nadir* (History of Shah Nadir) students were often exposed to a modicum of history.

The musical comedy *O Olmasin, Bu Olsin* (If not that bride, then this one), written by Uzeyir Hajibeyov in 1911, makes humorous reference to *Tarikhi-Nadir*. One of the main characters, the merchant Mashadi Ibad, comments on how his friend sprinkles his conversation with pretentious words and phrases in Turkish, French, and Russian. "I've read nearly half of the *Tarikhi-Nadir*," says Mashadi Ibad, "but I still can't figure out what you're trying to say!"[18] The fact that the history text was so small makes the statement even more trenchant.

Underground Tunnels

There used to be several underground tunnels beneath the Old City. Several of these were constructed in the fifteenth century by the Shirvanshahs to serve as escape routes from the palace complex.

One underground tunnel was built by Gatir Haji Zeynalabdin at the beginning of the twentieth century to connect two of his residencies—one that used to stand where the Encyclopedia Building is now, and the other on what is now Aziz Aliyev Street. Haji wanted his family to be able to move easily between both houses, which were approximately one hundred meters apart and separated by the citadel wall. One of Haji's granddaughters told me that she often used this tunnel during her youth.

During the Bolshevik Revolution, most of the owners of these grand residences that included tunnels either fled the city or were killed. Their houses were usually

---

18. Alakbarov, "Baku's Old City," 38–45.

subdivided into many smaller apartments and the tunnels simply forgotten until the 1970s when archaeological work began in the Old Town.

Sports

One of the Old City's main entertainment areas was the Zorkhana, a stadium where athletic competitions took place. The Zorkhana dates back to at least the fifteenth century. Although few people know about it, this underground vault was located just a few steps beyond the Bukhari and Multani caravanserais, toward the Maiden Tower.

As at sports clubs of today, men paid an entrance fee to participate in various competitions, which included weightlifting, wrestling, and boxing. Contests were often accompanied by a trio of musicians playing traditional instruments such as the *kamancha,* the *zurna,* and the *naghara* (string, wind, and percussive instruments). Unfortunately, many of the traditional melodies that accompanied the sports have long since been forgotten. Only one, by the name of *Jangi* (Warlike) is still performed prior to the opening of national wrestling competitions. The Zorkhana also functioned as a fitness club. When no organized competitions were taking place, men went there to do exercises and use the equipment.

Young men could test their strength against professional wrestlers who came from Tabriz, Ardabil, Sarab, and other cities of Southern Azerbaijan. Huseyngulu Sarabski wrote of a wrestler nicknamed Atliaylig Abdulali (Six-month Abdulali), who took on each and every contender in the arena, one by one. Before each match the renowned musician Haji Zeynal Agha Karim would sing a song glorifying Abdulali, who would then untie his belt, toss his hat into the arena, and jump onto the stage with a wide grin. Younger hopefuls would approach him, and Abdulali would quickly dispense with them. When Abdulali's task was complete, the spectators would toss in rubles in denominations of three, five, or even ten rubles—a considerable amount of money at the time.

Other competitions held at the Zorkhana included lifting, hurling, and catching heavy millstones. This last event was referred to as Mil Oyunu (Millstone game). Participants were usually accompanied by a *naghara* (drum) player who gradually increased the tempo by beating the drum faster and faster.

Poetry Readings and Musical Competitions

Baku residents also enjoyed attending poetry readings (*sheir majilslari*) and performances of a popular style of music, called *mugam,* which is a type of Oriental modal style music (*mugam akhshamlari*). Poets, musicians, and other performers often gathered together to recite *rubai* and *gazals* (lyrical verses) and listen to *mugam.* Performances were nearly always accompanied by abundant refreshments of sweets and tea.

PHENOMENE CINEMA AND CASINO
Designed by J. K. Ploshko and finished by 1912, it is now the State Puppet Theater.

The Duma and Nikolayevskaya Street.

Residents of Icheri Sheher also enjoyed *meykhana,* an improvisational musical/
literary form indigenous to Baku and its surrounding villages. *Meykhana* competitions are popular to this day despite being almost drowned out during Soviet
times for being too politically controversial.

Meykhana (literally, "wine houses") derived their name from Oriental-style
pubs where these performances historically took place. Contests involved two or
more poets exchanging verses back and forth extemporaneously, and often joking
or disparaging in tone. This early predecessor to modern-day rap often touched
upon social and political issues of the day. At the end of each contest, the audience
would decide which poet had proven the cleverest or issued the most elegant turn
of phrase, and would declare him the winner.

Entertainments

Another favorite pastime among the youth of old Baku was raising pigeons. The
birds were kept in dovecotes on the roofs of homes. Each morning the owners
would clamor up the roof, feed their flock, and then whistle loudly to propel them
off into flight. Even today, one can find pigeon lovers in the Inner City.

Nard (backgammon) was (and still is) a favorite game of the Inner City. Each
family had a set and the men would often sit and play the game for hours. Some
also played *shatranj* (chess) and *dama* (checkers).

Cartoon of a zealot trying to obstruct the way to school for female students.

Children played various games such as *chumrug-chumrug, besh-onbesh, usta shagird, dash-bash, gizlanpach* (hide-and-seek), *oghru-oghru, shumagadar,* and many others that are now forgotten. Of these games only *gizlanpach* is still popular today. *Banovsha* (red rover) also remains a perennial favorite.

Cuisine

Inner City dwellers had a propensity for eating meat and often referred to it as *jan* (life). Once an elderly inhabitant recited an old proverb to me: "Go to the market and buy *jan* ["life"–specifically, "meat"]. If *jan* is not available, buy *yarimjan* ["half-life," or "eggs"]. If *yarimjan* cannot be found, buy *badimjan* ["eggplant," otherwise known as "the poor man's food"].

Certain dishes were typical of the Old City and the surrounding villages, such as *dushbara* (soup with tiny lamb dumplings), *shorgogal* (a rounded cookie flavored with salt and spices), and *chudu* (a puff pastry stuffed with mincemeat and sprinkled with sugar and sumac). These dishes were not typically prepared in other parts of the country. The *pakhlava* (bakhlava) of Baku is also quite specific and differs from the Turkish and Lebanese varieties.

Khash and *kalla-pacha* (head and legs) were also famous dishes in old Baku. On nearly all holiday mornings, men would meet their friends in special cafés called *khashkhana* where they partook of *khash,* a hearty, thick soup made with calfs' or sheeps' feet and heavily seasoned with vinegar and chopped garlic. Eating *khash* with friends remains a popular activity to this day.

Prior to Baku's becoming part of the Russian Empire, Muslims in Baku almost never partook of alcoholic beverages, as they were banned by Islam. Nevertheless, some forms of wine (*mey, sharab,* and *chakhir*) were occasionally served at poetry readings or musical performances. Hard spirits were almost entirely unknown. Naturally, with the coming of the Russians, vodka became ubiquitous. Azerbaijanis began to drink vodka, although usually moderately. Public drunkenness within the native community was a rarity. Local varieties of vodka were *üzüm arağı* (grape vodka), *zoğal arağı* (corn vodka), and *tut arağı* (mulberry vodka).

Traditional Hats

Azerbaijanian men traditionally sported the national hat (*papag*) and a mustache. Until the early twentieth century it was considered shameful to appear on the street without both, although westernized citizens had already begun to flout the rules. Sometimes when men were involved in a serious argument, they would threaten, "I'll cut off your mustache!" Likewise, the hat also symbolized a man's honor. If someone touched a man's hat, or, God forbid, grabbed it off his head, it was considered a great affront, possibly resulting in bloodshed.

Charitable Works

During all religious holidays, the wealthy and even the middle classes would organize an *ehsan* or charity dinner for the poor. This entailed opening the doors of all homes. On the first floor, long tables were loaded with various hot dishes and sweets. Anyone could come in from the street and eat as much as they liked. Servants would take away the empty plates and bring more. Hundreds of houses provided *ehsan* during the holidays. Sometimes merchants would place charity tables in front of their shops.

Should someone prove too eager to get something for nothing, there was a saying:

> *Bu saninchun Ehsan deyil.*
> It's not an Ehsan for you.

Gochus

The *gochus* were the bullies or gangsters of the Inner City. With glowering expressions and long mustaches, these arrogant figures dressed in national "costumes and were usually armed to the hilt with guns and daggers. As they walked through the streets, no one dared to confront them no matter how outrageous their behavior. *Gochus* appeared around the end of the nineteenth century as a response to the Georgian gangsters called *kintos* who were engaged in kidnapping, robbing, and threatening Baku's wealthier denizens.

94

Baku railway station, 1915.

Originally meant to protect, *gochus* themselves began to be feared very much. Baku's police network was simply unable to deal with the *kintos,* leaving the wealthy to take matters into their own hands, which they did by recruiting and training an entire class of bodyguards. The *gochus* did rid Baku of the *kintos,* but by that time they themselves had become a force to be reckoned with. Millionaires found plenty of reason to keep them around; whenever they were involved in an argument, they would send their *gochus* to fight for them, often resulting in a duel. Over time, *gochus* began to band together and form a kind of mafia.[19]

Manaf Suleymanov wrote that a group of *gochus* once kidnapped the famous Baku millionaire Agha Musa Naghiyev, who was known as a miser. The *gochus* demanded ten thousand gold rubles for his release and threatened to carve him up into little pieces. Agha Musa firmly replied, "I can pay only 1,000 rubles. Of course, you can cut me up into little pieces, but then you won't get anything at all." The *gochus* understood that Agha Musa would rather die than part with his ten thousand rubles, and so they released him for the ransom he had negotiated.[20]

19. Suleymanov, *Memories about Things*, 33-35.
20. Ibid, 75-76.

Not all *gochus* were gangsters or armed mercenaries who worked for the ruling elite. Some were wealthy young men simply looking for adventure. Often they ended up quarreling with one another or threatening unwary passersby. However, there were "good *gochus*" too. *Gochus* helped to save the Inner City during the Armenian and Bolsheviik massacre of March 1918, as they were the only armed Azerbaijanis around.

Businessman Teymur Ashurbeyov, who lived in the Outer City, and Mammad Hanifa Taghiyev of the Inner City, mobilized their *gochus,* who then rallied and armed numerous other citizens. Together, these newly formed troops went to meet the Armenian Dashnak military forces. As a result, the Inner City and several streets of the Outer City were spared the main effects of the massacre.

Mulberry Tree

There used to be a very large ancient mulberry tree just behind the Juma Mosque in the Inner City. On hot summer days, men would sit under it playing *nard* and drinking tea. The tree was such a well-known landmark that people used to say, "Let's meet at the Mulberry Tree" or "I live left of the Mulberry Tree." A popular song was even written about this tree as a symbol of the Inner City.

Sometime in the 1980s the tree was cut down during a construction project, causing a great deal of upset among the local inhabitants. Some months later, someone decided to plant a new mulberry tree in its place. With the increased rate of turnover of the Inner City's inhabitants, however, no one can even remember the significance of the original mulberry tree, and now this new one has been cut down, too.

In short, the history of the Inner City during the first oil boom (1850–1920) is extremely rich. The reminiscences of Huseyngulu Sarabski and Manaf Suleymanov, as well as the stories of the elderly Inner City residents, combined with old newspaper and magazine accounts, provide a nuanced trove of materials revealing an intriguing and complex social and architectural history. Now that Azerbaijan is fully established as a nation in its own right, today's historians are confronted with the enormous task of going back to these original sources, mining them for the truth, and setting forth an objective account of our country's history once and for all.

Advertisement for "Nobel Brothers Soap," 1910.

№ 1 Вокзалъ. Баку.
La Gare. Bakou.

The Station.

Nicholas Perevoshchikov's guidebook "Baku in My Pocket," 1909.

Баку, Городской садъ
Bacou, Jardin de ville.
A. W. N.

City garden.

Carpet cleaning.

Парапетъ — Parapète   Баку — Bakou

Parapet.

The water vendor.

Summer club.

Татарская религіозная мистерія : Шахсей-Вахсей.   Баку.

La fête Schachsei-Wachsei.   Bacou.

The Schachsei Wachsei Festival.

Baku— The Oil City and Its People

TADEUSZ SWIETOCHOWSKI

———

The Oil Revolution and the Opening to the World

Azerbaijan: the origin of this name is often traced back to the Persian word *azer*, meaning "fire." Azerbaijan, named "Land of Fire" for its numerous Zoroastrian temples whose eternal flames are fed by the local oil sources. The extraction of this fuel dates back to prehistoric times, yet for centuries, Azerbaijan was better known as a transportation corridor along the Caspian coast. This changed swiftly following the country's incorporation into the Russian Empire in the early nineteenth century.

After decades of stagnation, the extraction of oil began to gain momentum in 1859, when the first kerosene refineries were built in Baku and neighboring villages. The turning point, however, came as the result of a governmental act—the most consequential ever issued in Azerbaijan by the Russian bureaucracy under the Tsardom. In 1872 the practice of granting oil concessions on state land was replaced by long-term leases to the highest bidders, throwing the door wide open to natives, Russians, and especially foreign investors with substantial capital and the inclination to engage in large-scale mechanized oil farming.

Within a year of this reform, the old laborious process of well digging was replaced by the new mechanized method of drilling, and a spectacular gusher inaugurated the rise of Baku to the position of a major world-scale oil-producing center. "For a long time the Eastern part of Trans-Caucasia was regarded as almost plague-infested," writes Hasan bey Zardabi, founder of the first Azeri-language newspaper *Akinchi* (*Ploughman*):

> Then, in the rocky fields around Baku, oil fountains shot up high, and everybody watched these marvelous phenomena of nature with distinct fascination. As the owners of the fountains quickly piled up their millions, capital and expertise began to flow in from everywhere. What used to be in effect the place of administrative exile now began to bubble with life.[1]

Although at the middle of the century Baku was still a sleepy port town, with the influx of Western investment funds and technology during Russia's Great Reforms period in the 1870s, the city went through rapid changes. This inflow of industry and new revenue turned Baku into a quintessential boom city, with the highest rate of population increase in the Russian Empire, reaching 112,000 inhabitants in 1897, and almost a quarter of a million in 1913.[2]

The ripple effects of this growth led to almost revolutionary transformations, albeit within a geographically limited sphere: it generated employment for tens

1. Kaspiy (daily newspaper, 1899), 212.
2. For a history of Baku, see Ashurbeyli, S., *Istoriia goroda Baku*; and Badalov, R., "Baku: gorod i strana," 256–79 in Furman, D. E., *Azerbaidzhan i Rossiia. Obshchestva i.gosudarstva*, Moskva, 2001, 256–79; On the urban growth of Baku, see Altstadt, Audrey, *The Azerbaijani Turks: Power and Identity under Russian Rule,* Hoover Institution Press, 1992, 20–49.

The Bibi-Heybat Mosque.

of thousands of nonagricultural workers; it created such attributes of economic modernization as labor migrations and the advent of railroad and steamship transportation; and it brought about the rise of an urban metropolis, Baku. The overall effect of the oil revolution was a dichotomy not uncommon for a colonial situation: a generally traditional economy contrasting with a rapidly expanding industry based on mineral resources rather than manufacturing, and was geared toward the needs of external markets. Azerbaijan's relationship to oil would become similar to that of Egypt and the Suez Canal—"sometimes a blessing, sometimes a curse"—and for most foreigners oil remained the primary object of interest in the country.

The chief foreign investor in Baku oil was the Nobel Brothers Company, founded by Robert and Immanuel Nobel. Gradually, the company took over ownership of nearly half of the local oil production.[3] The Parisian Rothschild family, another major foreign investor, focused its efforts on the crucial problem of how to transport crude oil to the world markets. In 1883 construction was completed on the railroad line between Baku and Batumi along the coast of the Black Sea. This groundbreaking investment in transportation was followed by the laying down of pipelines, making Baku's oil more accessible to the global marketplace and expanding the country's business beyond selling solely to Russia.[4]

With the expansion of the oil industry, Baku grew into a thoroughly multinational urban center in which no single ethnic element was predominant. The three largest groups were the Russians, the Armenians, and the Muslims, the last of which held a plurality, usually hovering around 40 percent, although their statistical designation included the natives of Russia as well as those of Iran, Azerbaijan, Dagestan, and even the Volga Tatars. The Azeris were for the most part half-workers, half-peasants, and, of all the groups of inhabitants, were the most closely linked with their village background. If employed in the oil industry, they worked mainly as unskilled laborers. The better-paid jobs, requiring skill or training, were held by Russians

3. See, Tolf, R. W., *The Russian Rockefellers: The Saga of the Nobel Family and of the Russian Oil Industry,* Stanford University Press, 1976.
4. See, Suleymanov, M. *Neft Milyonjusu*, Baku, 1995; Ibragimov, M., *Predprinimatel'naia deiatel'nost' G. Z. Tagieva*, Baku, Elm, 1991.

or Armenians. Likewise, the municipal council had, by law, to be dominated by a Christian majority.

The city of Baku developed in concentric belts of population. The center, marked by the turn-of-the-century beaux arts architecture and the walled section of the Old Town Icheri Sheher, was inhabited by immigrants of European origin. Some of these inhabitants would go on to achieve worldwide fame in a variety of fields: writer Kurban Said, World War II Soviet superspy Richard Sorge, cellist Mstislav Rostropovich, Nobel Prize winner in physics Lev Landau, and chess master Garry Kasparov.

The Bakintsi, who were seen as a special layer of the city population and an exception to the general pattern, were a cosmopolitan mixture of individuals of mainly native origins. Like the middle-class Levantines of other Middle Eastern cities such as Alexandria, Cairo, Beirut, and Istanbul, the Bakintsi were a product of the contact between various civilizations within an urban environment, except that their language of expression was Russian rather than French.

Surrounding the city, in a residential zone where oil drilling and processing were prohibited, were the industrial suburbs. Here in the derrick-studded, heavily polluted landscape resided the majority of the native Azeri-Turkic inhabitants, many of which were immigrant laborers from Southern Azerbaijan or from across the Iranian border.

With its multilingual population, large size, and hectic pace of life, Baku was an alien enclave in Azerbaijan, known then as Eastern Transcaucasia. The city had an irresistible draw and attracted the most enterprising and educated people from all

Древняя крѣпостная стѣна.   БАКУ.

Г. Ш. Сахарянцъ. Баку.

The ancient city wall.

over the country, turning Baku into the virtual capital of Azerbaijan as well as the fountainhead of the rising native intelligentsia and entrepreneurial class. The oil boom allowed the Azeris—who had owned the oil wells, kerosene refineries, and real estate of Baku—to reap quick fortunes. In the very first stages of Baku's industrial expansion, which lasted until 1872, Azeris still controlled most oil-related enterprises. After the regulation on bidding leases went into effect, however, the natives began to lose out to their Armenian, Russian, and Western European competitors. Nevertheless, Azeri oil entrepreneurs such as the Diaghilev, Naghiyev, Assadulayev, Mukhtarov, and Sultanov families succeeded in accumulating great wealth while other Azeris gained wealth through real estate holdings.[5]

With the first economic boom of Baku came the introduction of the beaux arts and fin de siècle style of architecture, with the Philharmonic Hall and the surrounding neighborhood built as a visual monument to the city's prosperity. Despite Baku's thriving industry, the rapidly growing urban agglomeration at this time had gained a negative reputation as "the city without water" and was regarded by tourists as being one of the worst-run cities in the world, considering its wealth.[6]

5. Dastakian Nikita, *Il venait de la ville noire*, Paris, 1901, 35-36.
6. Villari, L., *The Fire and Sword in the Caucasus*, 181, London, 1906.

Ольгинская улица.   Баку.

Large, sandy canyons with no trace of vegetation surrounded Baku. Violent winds from the north brought penetrating dust, which, despite sealed double windows, still managed to cover furniture inside houses. In the summer, heat waves often reached over 120 degrees. Rains seldom fell, but every time they did, water flowed in from the surrounding canyons and flooded the city. Streets turned into rivers traversable only by sitting on the back of a *hambal*, a worker from Iran who would carry people, furniture, luggage, or purchases in exchange for a few kopecks.

Olga Street.

The city suffered from a shortage of potable water. Attempts to desalinate the water using distilling equipment proved to be insufficient for the rapidly growing population. The only solution was to construct a sixty-mile-long water pipeline from the Sholar Mountains to Baku.

The city's asphalt sidewalks, known as *kirs*, were usually in very bad condition. Oftentimes the *kirs* would turn soft in the heat, leaving the footprints of pedestrians. Horse-drawn streetcars were used as a means of transportation along the sides of major thoroughfares. These streetcars, contracted under a Belgian company, stopped anywhere along their route upon request.[7]

7. Kurban Said, *Ali and Nino,* 12. For a recent monograph on Kurban Said, see Reiss, T., *The Orientalist: Solving the Mystery of a Strange and Dangerous Life,* New York, 2005.

Despite its diversity, this vibrant industrial city did not turn into a cultural melting pot. Ethnic communities continued to live their separate lives in distinct neighborhoods, and differences in socioeconomic status perpetuated the division of culture, religion, and language.

The urban world of Baku soon gained a place in the world of literature. In the acclaimed Polish novel *Przedwiosnie* (Early spring), author Stefan Zeromski describes Baku as "the land of milk and honey" for immigrants from Poland, who, while resisting assimilation with Russia in their homeland, developed a relationship with Russia in the multicultural world of Baku. Zeromski knew of Baku only through secondhand experience and the stories told to him. Kurban Said, whose real name was Lev Nussimbaum, was a Jewish author who converted to Islam and a native of Baku. In his best-known novel, *Ali and Nino,* he describes the city:

> There were really two towns, one inside the other, like a kernel in a nut. Outside the Old Wall was the Outer City with wide streets, high houses; its people noisy and greedy for money. This Outer City was built because of the oil that comes from our desert and brings riches. There were theaters, schools, hospitals, libraries, policemen and beautiful women with naked shoulders. If there was a shooting in the Outer City, it was always over money. Europe's geographical border began in the Outer City. Inside the Old City the houses were narrow and curved like oriental daggers, Minarets pierced the mild moon, so different from the oil derricks the House of Nobel had erected.[8]

Said also explains the legendary origins of the city's most famous architectural monument, the Maiden Tower on the eastern wall of the Old City.

> Mehmed Yussuf Khan, ruler of Baku, had it built in honor of his daughter, whom he wanted to marry. The incestuous marriage was never consummated. The daughter threw herself from the tower while her love-crazed father was hurrying to her room. The stone on which the maiden fell to her death is referred to as the Virgin Stone. Sometimes, this stone is covered with flowers, the offering of a bride on the day before her wedding.[9]

The rate at which oil was being drilled grew at a faster pace than in any other region in the world, and by the end of the nineteenth century, the western coast of the Caspian Sea became the second-biggest oil exporter in the world, next to the United States. But the boom was not destined to continue unceasingly and began to fade toward the turn of the century.[10] Many factors led to this decline, the most obvious being the wasteful, uncontrolled exploitation of the oil fields. Another cause was competition from newly discovered oil resources, primarily

8. Ibid, 13.
9. Yergin, D., *Prize: The Epic Quest for Oil, Money and Power,* New York, Simon Schuster, 1991, 133.
10. *Ali and Nino*, 111.

in Iran, which led to a sharp downturn in the price of crude oil. With the decline of prosperity, Baku became the grounds of social and ethnic antagonisms. As its multiethnic population and economic differences coincided with ethnoreligious divisions, the city and its environs became the scene of internecine violence between the Azeris and the Armenians from 1905 to 1907 and, later, in 1918, when crisis hit the Russian statehood once more.

Geopolitics of Baku Oil

With the coming of the twentieth century, a new and crucial factor shaped the destiny of Baku, and its oil became the subject of international conflicts. Almost immediately after Ottoman Turkey joined World War I in late 1914, it launched a disastrous military offensive aimed at the Caspian Sea coast.

A fountain in flames at Bibi-Heybat.

In *Ali and Nino,* Kurban Said describes the views of the newly arising situation in the words of a prominent Azerbaijani statesman:

> "Yes," said a fat man with brilliant eyes and a long mustache, "everything will indeed be different after the war." This was Fath Ali Khan of Khoja, a lawyer by profession. We knew that he was always thinking about the People and their cause. "Yes," he added fervently, "and as everything will be different, we need not beg for anyone's favors. Whoever wins this war will come out of it weak and covered with wounds, and we, who will be neither weakened nor wounded, will be in a position to demand, not to beg. We are an Islamic, a Shi'ite country, and we expect the same from the House of Romanov as from the House of Osman. Independence is everything that concerns us! And the weaker the great powers are after the war, the nearer is freedom for us. This freedom will come from us, from our unspent strength, from our money and our oil. For do not forget: the world needs us more than we need the world."[11]

Only in 1918, in the last months of the war, were the foreign armies able to seize the city. After the new wave

11. See, Suny, R., *The Baku Commune. 1917-1918: Class and Nationality in the Russian Revolution,* Princeton University Press, 1972; Swietochowski, T., *Russia and Azerbaijan, A Borderland in Transition,* Columbia University Press, 1995.

The Branobel Oil Company in Baku, 19th-20th century, unknown artist, oil on canvas, 71 × 42 cm (Provenance: The Nobel Family).

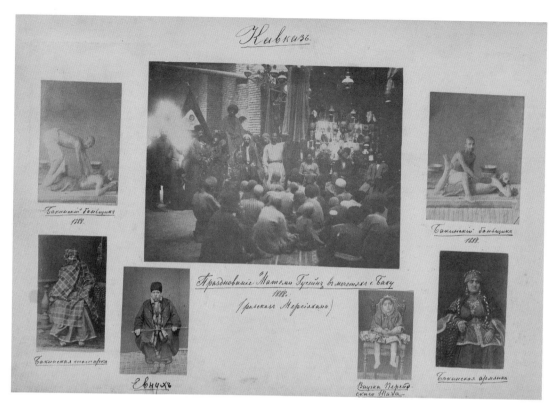

of Armenian-Muslim ethnic clashes in the March Days, the city was seized by the Bolshevik dictatorship, forming the Baku Commune. The goal of the commune was to impose upon Baku a unifying peace between the warring ethnicities. The commune was abolished after only three months of existence by the Russian Socialist Revolutionaries, who were eager to invite the British forces to help defend the city from the approaching Ottoman army. Despite the efforts of the revolutionaries, Baku fell into the hands of the Ottoman Empire in mid-September, followed shortly by an outbreak of anti-Armenian violence in retaliation of the March Days. By this time, the rest of Azerbaijan had proclaimed its independence in May 1918, and the capital had been moved to Ganja, only to be moved back to Baku under Ottoman occupation. The Republic of Azerbaijan remained under Ottoman rule for several weeks before being vanquished by the British late in 1918.[12]

On April 28, 1920, after the attack of a task force of Soviet armored trains that had been ordered by Lenin to take possession of the city while leaving the oil fields intact, Baku was seized. The Independent Republic of Azerbaijan ceased to exist. Unlike in the countryside, there was no resistance to the invasion in the culturally

Clockwise from the top center: mourning of Imam Hussein in Baku Mosque, 1888; Baku bath house, 1888; Armenian woman; granddaughter of Persian shah; eunuch; Tatar woman in Baku; Baku bath house, 1888.

12. See Liber, G., "Korenizatsiia: Restructuring Soviet Nationality Policy in the 1920s," *Ethnic and Racial Studies 1*, 1991.

Husseyngulu Sarabski
Performing the role of Majnun in the first
Muslim opera, *Leyli and Majnun,* staged in
Baku in January 1908.

diverse city, of which the Azeri accounted for less than half of the population. Appreciating the distinct character of Baku, the Communist Party head of Azerbaijan, Sergei Kirov, considered having just the city transferred from Azerbaijani jurisdiction to that of Soviet Russia.

National Identity in the Multiethnic City

Recognizing Baku's distinct character, Moscow decided to implement the policy of *korenizatsia* (indigenization), a form of social contract offering the use of native language, growth of education, and native bureaucracy. As a method of achieving the harmonious coexistence of nationalities within the Soviet regime, *korenizatsia* called for the full equality of minority languages and Russian.[13]

In the early stages of the *korenizatsia* policy, the "nationalistically deviated" Communists called for a rapid increase of the native element among the Baku proletariat, which was ethnically still a largely foreign body. Russian and other nonnative workers who could not be made to leave Azerbaijan were now required to learn the native language of the country, Azeri. Such a proposal was met with anger and rejection from the party leadership.[14] The requirement that all residents learn the native language went into effect only after the influx of local labor under the industrialization of the 1930s saw the proportion of Azeri workers grow into a majority. Yet its application became notorious for its lackadaisical enforcement, as very few of those who actually did take the required instruction reached a level of proficiency in the language.

Even though knowledge of Russian was more common among the local elite than among the masses, it offered the prospect of democratization as well as educational revolution among the predominantly illiterate population. Within the intelligentsia, literary and artistic associations flourished, as did feminist groups such as Bayramov, which promoted the equal rights of women. Members of the intelligentsia pursued aspirations of enlightenment and modernization, establishing new schools and publishing books and newspapers all in the style of a newly emerging literary dialect free of foreign influence.

Modern theater, a field in which Azerbaijan has been a pioneer in the Middle East since the years of Mirza Fathali Akhundov in the mid-nineteenth century, progressed from the epoch of amateurish shows to an era of more polished productions, with professional teams performing in major towns. Translations of world-renowned classic plays gained popularity, as did works of contemporary Azeri playwrights such as Husein Javid, Samad Vurgun, and Jabbar Jabbarli.

13. For a comprehensive review of the alphabet reform issue, see Baldauf, I., *Schriftreform und Schriftwechsel bei den Muslimischen Russland und Sowjetturken (1850–1937). Ein Symptom ideengeschichtlicher und kulturpolitischen Entwicklungen,* Budapest, Akademiai Kiado, 1993.
14. Zemtsov, I., *Partiia ili mafia?,* Paris, 1970, 66.

B. Kaabak, poster from the Baku Fair, 1925, lithograph.

Poster of the newspaper *Baku Worker*, 1925, lithograph.

Baku, view from the sea, 1887.

A quarter of a century after the performance of the first Azerbaijani opera, *Leyli and Majnun,* composed by Uzeir Hajibeyli, the State Theater of Opera and Ballet was opened to the public in Baku.

The birth and growth of Azerbaijani filmmaking also began to show promise around this time. In tune with the belief that people in the East are better accustomed to persuasion through images than through arguments, the cinema became a powerful means of mass propaganda. The number of movie houses increased from seven in 1920 to more than four hundred in the span of only two decades. Filmmakers would put forward a message of respect for the Communist Party's principle of infusing socialist ideas with their own native style, but in the films of the 1920s it was this native style that dominated over Soviet content.

Foreign visitors to Azerbaijan around this time were impressed by the extent to which *korenizatsia* had affected the literal appearance of the country–billboards in the native Azeri had replaced those in Russian. Still, the process was not all-encompassing, for the telephone and postal services as well as medical institutions and technical training continued to rely on Russian.

The age of *korenizatsia* also ushered in a cultural revolution, partly by replacing the Arabic alphabet, which was unsuitable for the phonetic systems of Turkic languages, with the Latin alphabet. This change occurred in 1926 and was mirrored two years later in Kemalist Turkey.[15] In Soviet Azerbaijan, the Latinization of the alphabet gave a powerful impetus to the struggle against illiteracy, and the effects were soon visible. By 1931 almost a third of the population was able to read, compared with only one-fourth in 1926, and by 1933 more than half the population was literate. By then a policy of obligatory universal education had been imposed, an act that ultimately significantly reduced illiteracy.

During the eventful decade of the 1930s, Soviet criticisms of *korenizatsia* began to multiply. With the victory of the Socialist revolution, the argument went, the Russian language was no longer a tool for the oppression of non-Russian peoples. Rather, it became the means of introducing those peoples to Russian culture. *Korenizatsia* was not considered an absolute value in and of itself, and the term

15. Badalov, "Baku: Gorod i strana," op. cit., 272–73.

dropped out of usage. Similarly, the Latin alphabet ceased to be used after 1940, when Cyrillic replaced it, in the new spirit of a linguistic Russianization that was a prerequisite for success in Soviet society.

The Alexander Embankment, Baku, 1887.

Perspective view of Olgina & Mikhailov Streets, 1887.

    Even though in the 1920s and '30s Baku continued to supply the Soviet Union with oil and its products, and experienced further urban growth, the term "boom" was no longer applicable to the condition of its planned economy. Caspian oil fueled the Soviet Union's five-year plans during the 1930s, as well as their defense efforts during World War II. The geopolitical dimension of the security of the Baku oil fields reemerged, just as in 1918, but on a scale incomparably larger given the context of a new world conflict. In the first two years of the war, during which the Soviet Union maintained its neutrality, the British and French high commands drafted plans for destroying the Baku oil installations via air raids from Syria and Iraq, with an aim of stopping deliveries to Germany that were the result of agreements between Moscow and Berlin. These plans were never executed, however, as France surrendered in the summer of 1940. After the Russians entered the war, the Caucasus region supplied most of their oil and oil products.

The Golden Age of the Bakintsi

The war years brought a new influx of city residents, many resettling from other parts of the Soviet Union. Another, larger, wave of newcomers included former wartime servicemen who preferred to settle in the capital or its suburbs instead of returning to their native villages. As a result of Baku's population growth, in the 1960s the city built underground mass transit between the center of Baku and the outlying regions. The city center, some of its buildings having been constructed by German POWs, no longer evoked images of the urban chaos left by foreign visitors at the turn of the century. Rather, the coastal parks, boulevards, and even some older buildings invited comparisons with Chicago—perhaps partly because the winds blow through both cities with a similar strength.

As in many Soviet cities, the principle of façade remained in full force. Outside of the center, in the new Khrushchev-style residential sections of the city, a third of the population lived at a density of ten square meters per person. As a dissident writer noted, on the basis of Soviet statistical data,

> In Azerbaijan are more residential buildings without water, electricity, and sanitation than in all of Western Europe. Elsewhere, the old-time slums spread. Some sections, especially those with ethnically mixed populations, were crime ridden. The crime rate in the 1960s was three times higher than in Moscow, and the number of drug takers two to three times higher, and there were twice as many cases of venereal diseases. The problems of Azerbaijan were primarily irreversible poverty, lawlessness, and lack of hope. The average income was 1.7 times lower than in Moscow, and the number of unqualified workers 1.8 times higher.[16]

In line with the economic trends of the time, which reduced Baku's resources to the level of strategic reserve, the city experienced a slow and steady outflow of its Armenian (and, to a lesser extent, Russian) population.

After decades of Soviet rule, the golden age of Baku oil was fading into history. When Turkey joined the North Atlantic Treaty Organization alliance, the Baku oil fields found themselves within the reach of potential enemy air forces and, later, midrange missiles. Beyond the less-than-ideal geopolitical situation, the additional causes of this decline were exhaustion due to intensive exploitation, and, more crucially, underinvestment in the search for new deposits deeper in the sea. As Baku's oil-producing regions were sinking into decline, new deposits in the northern part of the Caspian Sea, such as at Tenghiz in Kazakhstan, were expanding their production. Thus, the center of Soviet oil extraction shifted toward the Volga basin and the Urals. Exploitation of oil resources began in the Siberian region of Tyumen during the 1960s, and then in Siberia, with its great resources but high transportation costs. Meanwhile, in Baku and its environs, the easily accessible but largely exhausted onshore deposits passed into the category of "long-term reserves." However, Azerbaijan retained its position as the main producer of equipment for oil extraction in the Soviet Union.

Despite all of this, Baku not only survived the decline of the oil extraction industry but kept growing, with the energy of its urbanization process, which was reinforced by nonoil investment funds from the Center, as Moscow used to be called. During World War II the population of Azerbaijan's capital had grown with the influx of refugees and settlers from Russia. Many of them had come after

Baku porter.

16. Gasanly Dzhamil, "Natsional'nyi vopros v Azerbaidzhane, Pravda i vymysel (1956–1959 gg)," *Zerkalo*, 6/6, 2006, no. 81, 33.

the evacuation of Russian institutions and industrial establishments, and thus were well educated. Their presence had an effect on both the ethnic composition of the city and its Russian culture. Some of these wartime newcomers contributed to the flourishing of the Bakintsi social environment in the post-Stalinist decades of the 1960s and 1970s, as the vision emerged of the Bakintsi as a virtually separate nationality, very distinct from those Azeris who were not city dwellers.

In the words of a Baku historian, "It would be very difficult to provide an exact definition of the Bakintsi, if not outright impossible. Such factors as language, ethnic origins, and social status appeared as a particular lifestyle in their urban manners, even in their clothes." The underlying factors that generated the Bakintsi lifestyle are equally incredibly hard to identify. Obviously one factor was the effect of the Soviet thaw and the resulting neophyte discovery of world culture, including the emergence of Hemingwayan and Remarqueian mannerisms among the city's youth. Other, specifically Bakintsi causes could be noted: the mixture of cultures in the historically short time frame, which sharpened the Bakintsi's receptiveness to cultural diversity; the mobility and dynamism of the Baku way of life, which encouraged quick adaptation to changing conditions; and the typical Bakuvian inclination to friendliness, in which everyone knew everyone as they circulated at not-very-large city promenades.

Laundry washing at the port, 1887.

The aura of city life was cosmopolitan, and Russian-speaking, and the new openness to world culture stimulated in Baku, as throughout the Soviet Union, a search for "roots" and a new vision of national culture. Cosmopolitanism and weak ties to the national history and national culture affected a generation—particularly those who continued to identify themselves as Bakintsi. Many ended up as émigrés, taking with them the image of the city, the likeness of which they said could not be found elsewhere. Others, in time, became like "old-age teenagers, enclosed in their past, and distancing themselves strictly from any movements of the present time."[17]

The language controversy was renewed in post-Stalinist Azerbaijan. According to a new law implemented throughout the Soviet Union, the teaching of native languages ceased to be obligatory in Russian schools. However, the choice of sending their children to either a Russian or a native school was still left up to

Baku Arba carriage, 1887.

17. Ibid.

116 A leaf from the album "In Memory of the Fiftieth Anniversary of Immanuel Ludvigovich Nobel, June 10, 1909."

the parents. When Imam Mustafayev's Azerbaijani government, fearing linguistic Russianization, attempted to delay implementation of the law in order to reaffirm Azeri as the official language of the country, a political crisis arose at the highest level of the party hierarchy. In the words of Mustafayev's rival, Veli Akhundov:

> The issue of recognizing Azeri as the official language of the republic in 1956 brought negative consequences such as a reawakening of nationalist sentiments and distortions in Party policies. The issue was exploited by various demagogues and nationalists for the purpose of heating up nationalist passions, especially among students and parts of the intelligentsia.

In response to such criticism, writer and former Stalin Prize recipient Mir Ibrahimov, in reference to the postal service's refusal of telegrams and letters in Azeri, said, "Some comrades show not only dislike but contempt for the language of Azerbaijan.... I felt compelled to speak about such things, as people were turning to me with complaints." In June 1959 Mustafayev was forced into retirement due to perceived failures in his work, most notably the "confusion in the question of language."[18] The Moscow language policy was accepted, with the approval of well-educated Azeris whose personal ambitions and expectations reached beyond

18. Furman, D. Abasov, A. *Azerbaidzhanskaia revoliutsia,* op. cit, 123. Hasanli, J., "Natsional'nyi vopros v Azerbaidzhane," 33. See also Landau, Jacob, M., Kellner-Heinkele, Barbara, *Politics of Language in the Ex-Soviet Muslim States,* University of Michigan Press, 2001, 131.

the limits of their home country, and who favored the adoption of the Soviet lingua franca over the native tongue.

The complex interplay of the conquered people's national sentiments and imperial assimilation prompted an Azerbaijani historian to comment:

> The Soviet regime in Azerbaijan, as in other national republics, left its impact on the formation of national consciousness in a convoluted and contradictory manner. On the one hand, it promoted the idea of the Azerbaijani nation, and even cultivated highly incomplete Azerbaijani patriotism (incomplete inasmuch as the Azerbaijani culture was purposefully separated from its historic roots through such means as the imposition of atheism; the change of the Arabic alphabet to Latin, and then to Cyrillic; banning the normal study of the Musavatist period and of the links to the culture of the Iranian Azeri and akin peoples, Iranians and Turks; and inasmuch as any manifestation of patriotism had to be accompanied with swearing of friendship and fidelity to the Russian "older brother"). On the other hand, there was partly imposed and partly spontaneous Russianization. Characteristically, the process reached an especially large scale when Azerbaijani bureaucrats came into positions of power on multiple levels, squeezing out the non-Azeris. In the 1960s and '70s the number of Russian schools in Baku exceeded that of Azeri schools, even though the city was developing a greater Azeri character as a result of its ethnic composition. Both the intelligentsia and the bureaucrats sent their children mainly to Russian schools.[19]

It could be perceived that the bureaucrats and the intelligentsia together formed the bulk of what was the Soviet equivalent of a middle class. The long-term effect of this was a widening of the division between the inhabitants of the major cities and those of small towns and villages. The inhabitants of the rural regions of Azerbaijan felt that it was a waste of time to learn Russian, as it would never be used by local people and thus would be forgotten.

The Change of the Ethnic Environment

By the end of the Soviet era, Baku produced less than 3 percent of the Soviet Union's oil,[20] and its derricks looked like part of a museum exhibition from the time of the Nobel brothers. Lack of national independence was seen as a cause of the premature exhaustion of the onshore oil deposits, and it also limited—or in some cases precluded entirely—gains in the world market. In the later Soviet years, the Azerbaijani oil industry was thrown into deep decline, and the country

---

19. Yergin, *Prize,* op. cit., 774.
20. On the labor migration in the post-Soviet space, see Zaionchkovskaia, Z. (ed.), *Migratsiia i urbanizatsiia v SNG i Baltike v 90e gody,* Tsentr Izucheniia Problem Vynuzhdennoi Migratsii Stran SNG, Moskva, 1999.

found itself left with an underdeveloped infrastructure, a low standard of living, and inefficient and ecologically harmful alternative industries. Underlying all of this was the widespread but relatively hidden high level of unemployment, which affected roughly one-fifth of the labor force.

In the closing years of Soviet rule, Baku became a center of political upheaval. A major sign of unrest was the general strike organized in 1989 by the umbrella opposition group the People's Front of Azerbaijan. A violent shake-up came with the "Black January Days" of 1990, which were the last in a series of outbreaks of ethnic violence that had begun almost a century before. There followed a massive exodus of urban residents, primarily Armenians (330,000) and Russians (220,000), as well as thousands of Bakintsi.

This migration outward was matched by a reverse trend of incoming refugees and displaced persons from Nagorno-Karabakh and other Armenian-occupied territories, and from the Republic of Armenia itself. The influx of new inhabitants, almost all of whom were ethnic Azeri Turks, led to an inevitable change in Baku's urban composition. The city, whose tone had predominately been set by the Russian-speaking population, experienced a process well known in other Middle Eastern capitals a generation or two earlier—a rapid cultural-linguistic indigenization. While in the Levantine Arab cities the catalysts of change were Palestinian refugees, in Baku a comparable role was played by those displaced by the Nagorno-Karabakh War, and an overwhelming majority had rural backgrounds. This influx into Baku of a countryside population that was not used to city life caused friction with the established inhabitants, a situation worsened by housing shortages. Some of the refugees took over the more desirable residences of the former Armenian inhabitants in the center of the city, but were often evicted and relocated to the periphery, where most of the displaced persons were concentrated. Over time, and with no end to the refugee situation in sight, the newcomers slowly began to integrate into the city community.

The arrival of the Karabakh war refugees unfortunately coincided with the crisis in Azerbaijan's economy, which was one of the most severe and long lasting of all of the republics of the dissolved Soviet Union. Between 1991 and 1995 Azerbaijan's national income fell by more than half. While some of the major causes for the downturn were not economic (notably the Nagorno-Karabakh conflict), other factors had their roots deep in the economic system of the Soviet epoch. The disruption of the extensive commercial ties with other countries of the former Soviet Union significantly damaged a large part of the state-owned manufacturing sector. In 1994 Azerbaijan entered a state of hyperinflation, and prices rose month to month by up to 50 percent.

Despite the signs of decline in the Soviet regime, the use of Russian as a language among the Azeris in Baku continued throughout the last years of the Soviet Union, and among those who did not identify as Bakintsi. One particular

attraction of Russian was its facility in expressing and communicating the particulars of contemporary science and technology, as well as its function as a lingua franca for communicating with other ethnic groups of the Soviet Union. With regard to the question of Azerbaijani self-identification, the language element has never been clearly and unambiguously defined. What is known, though, is that many dissidents opposed to the Soviet rule used the Russian language, comparing themselves to the Algerian nationalists who utilized the French language in their struggle against French colonialism.

Shortly after the temporary decline of Russian in the first few years of post-Soviet independence, use of the language grew once more. The unchallengeable effect of Moscow television was an important influence, but so was the massive, if often temporary, migration of labor to Russia. This brought the language out into the distant Baku provinces, the traditional bastions of the Azeri Turkic.

Pre- and post-Soviet period postage stamps.

The language issue contained political potential, and in 2001 a decree by President Heydar Aliyev declared the usage and development of the native language to be one of the principal attributes of state independence of Azerbaijan. Subsequently, parliament passed legislation banning the use of Cyrillic in public places, and the streets of Baku became scenes of feverish activity as signs and billboards were changed. This third change to the country's alphabet proved incomparably more complex than the reform of the 1920s, when the majority of the population had been illiterate. The ban also caused dissatisfaction among the middle-aged and older sections of the public. Likewise, some opposition groups expressed concern that the enforced Latinization would reduce the readership of the independent press. Among the complaints about the reforms, the most frequent was that there was not much to read in the Latin script.

The Russian language continued to have an impact on Azerbaijan's educational system, and the number of Russian schools rose again, partly due to their

Баку. Биби-Эйбатъ.

Bibi-Heybat.

reputation for higher standards and the abundance of textbooks in Russian. On the broader spectrum of Baku's language situation, a local resident wrote:

> Despite all these changes, the Russian language is not dying out. Perhaps the younger generation tends to know Azeri better now, but the people who spoke Russian before the independence, regardless of their nationality, continue to speak it now, much like in the past.... When foreign films are shown on Azerbaijani channels, most of them are in Russian, not Azeri.... If I walk into a store and ask for something in Azeri, the sales assistant will answer me in Russian. My mother speaks Azeri on a very elementary level. She is now employed as a babysitter for an Azerbaijani family. The parents specifically hired a native-speaking Russian so that the child could learn Russian.[21]

The language debate entered the newspaper pages and became remarkably animated. In the view of the oppositionist magazine *Monitor*, the main tribune of Bakintsi, widespread use of the Russian language in the capital was

21. See "Alphabet and Language in Transition," *Azerbaijan International* 1 (Spring, 2000; special issue). Also, Landau, Kellner, op. cit.

a national-cultural phenomenon with a long history, stretching back to the time when Baku was the center of the oil industry and the fastest-growing city of the Russian empire. As it grew, the city increasingly withdrew from the rest of Azerbaijan and became the basis of the rising Baku subethnos of Russianized Azeris. These people accepted the Russian language as a means of acquiring a European education—a transition that they regarded as quite natural, given that the country's literary past was not so much Azeri as Persian.

This shift toward Europe eventually brought about a cultural division in Baku as Russianization became a negative sign of social mobility—even though Russian cultural traditions and mentality showed distrust of and isolationism toward Europe. Russianization was often connected to feelings of superiority and even snobbery, giving rise to what was called "linguistic apartheid." Europeanization through associations with Russia affected only some social groups, mostly those more wealthy and educated, and was therefore linked with the rise of the native middle class. According to the *Monitor,* this social group was distinguished by having a monthly income of between one hundred and one thousand dollars per family member. Such a category, however, included only a small fraction of the inhabitants of Azerbaijan, while the estimate of Russian-speaking Azeris living in Baku and other cities exceeded 1.5 million (close to 20 percent of the country's population). Politically, the Russian speakers did not form a pro-Russian element; rather they were oriented toward the West and, with time, toward integration with the European Union. Those that emigrated were, by comparison with other Azeris, more likely to move to Western countries than to Russia.

Gradually, the breakup of the Soviet Union was followed by the slow revival of the oil industry. Given the Contract of the Century signed in September 1994 between the government of Azerbaijan and a consortium of international companies, the door was once again wide open for Western investment and technology, and this time opened by the new post-Soviet republic of Azerbaijan.[22] Lamentably, the oil resources proved to be much less abundant than expected, largely due to Soviet-era overexploitation, while prices remained low for most of the 1990s. Once more, the subject of how to deliver the oil to world markets seemed as crucial as ever. Abiding by the wishes of their governments, Western companies insisted that the pipeline projects should bypass Russian territory and the overcrowded Turkish Straits.[23]

Faced with rising costs, the oil companies delayed their commitments, awaiting greater financial participation from those governments especially interested in the pipeline's construction namely, the United States, Turkey, Azerbaijan, and Georgia.

22. See Avakov, R. M., Lisov, A., *Rossia* i *Zakavkaz'e: realii nezavisimosti* i *novoe partnerstvo,* Moskva, Finanstatinform, 2000.
23. For an official Azerbaijani publication on the agreement, see *Century's Contract,* Baku, 1994.

Pre- and post-Soviet period postage stamps.

As a result, the final decision on routing the pipeline from Baku to the Mediterranean coast of Turkey was postponed for several years.

Just as during the late Soviet period, in the first decade of independence the percentage of the population that was unemployed remained high. The working-age population exceeded four million, of which only three-quarters were actually employed. By this time, labor migration was a national phenomenon and had been increasing since the late years of Soviet rule. This trend was reinforced by an exodus of Armenian and Russian residents from Baku, who accounted for a significant portion of the workforce—but they were replaced by Azeris who had acquired a sufficient level of training and experience.

As time passed, the urge to migrate spread to the unemployed and underemployed populations in the provinces, principally the war refugees. These moved straight to Baku, a city that could no longer absorb the growing mass of job seekers, despite the earlier departure of some residents. Unofficial labor markets, sometimes referred to as "slave markets," where the jobless found short-term employment at low pay, appeared, and even the employed searched for supplementary work. Many of the jobless began to move to Russia, mainly to Moscow and the surrounding areas, while others headed for Turkey and Iran. Estimates indicate that no less than 1.5 million Azeri immigrants, many of them temporary residents, currently live in Russia, mostly in the larger cities. In Moscow alone the number of Azeri immigrants is at least four hundred thousand, and in Saint Petersburg, two hundred thousand.[24] By contrast, the number immigrating to Turkey was not only much smaller but also consisted of many well-educated individuals. The Azeris who migrated to Turkey went via the Nakhchivan Autonomous Republic, and in the future this fact is likely to lead to a close mingling of the populations on both sides of the mere four-and-a-half-mile-long border between Azerbaijan and Turkey.

24. See: Avakov, R.M., Lisov, A., *Rossia i Zakavkaz'e: realii nezavisimosti i novoe partnerstvo,* Moskva, Finanstatinform, 2000

The Coming of the Second Oil Boom

The delayed construction of the Baku-Ceyhan pipeline was eventually completed, and an inauguration ceremony of the Azerbaijani section was held on May 25, 2005, at the Sangachal pumping station, twenty-five miles south of Baku. A carefully researched and well-planned and -executed project, the building of the pipeline was also an impressive feat of engineering. "The pipe dream turned into pipeline" was the saying of the day. Within a year, crude oil was flowing from the port of Ceyhan, feeding high incomes back into Azerbaijan. The pipeline became a solid foundation for the second boom, and at the same time weakened ties with Russia. "There is the feeling that Azerbaijani independence is now more sustainable," noted foreign visitors.

New discoveries of natural gas deposits balanced out the prospect of limited oil gains in the future. Moreover, the completion of the pipeline coincided with record-high prices of oil, and in the years that followed, projected gross national product growth was roughly 30 percent, among the highest in the world. However, public opinion polls indicated that few Azeris believed that a large proportion of the oil income would be used to significantly increase the standard of living; rather, they thought that it would disappear among the ruling elites. Nevertheless, by 2005 the average income had increased, the high poverty level had fallen somewhat, and a significant decline in unemployment was noticeable.[25]

The cover of the first issue of *Molla Nasreddin Magazine,* 1906.

The visual signs of the boom have been plentiful, and include new high-rise residential buildings, streets crowded with cars, and luxurious shops in the city center. In 2000 the old medieval section of Baku was included in the UNESCO list of global landmarks, alongside past monuments such as the palace of the local rules, the Shirvanshahs, and the Maiden Tower. Three years later, however, UNESCO also placed the Old City on the List of World Heritage in Danger, citing earthquake damage as well as poor conservation and questionable restoration efforts.

Baku's ambitions led to it join the competition for hosting the 2016 Olympic Games, with estimated costs of $20 billion, but ultimately the application was unsuccessful due to insufficient sports facilities, an underdeveloped tourist sector, and regional conflicts. Despite this, the city was given the right to reapply to

25. For discussions of the post-Soviet oil industry, see, Rasizade, A., "Azerbaijan, the U.S., and Oil Prospects on the Caspian Sea," *Journal of Third World Studies* XVI, No. 1, Spring 1991, 29-48; O'Lear, S., "Azerbaijan's Resource Wealth: Political Legitimacy and Public Opinion," *The Geographical Journal,* 173, no. 3, Sept. 2007, 207-23; Dzhuvarli, Togrul, "Azerbaidzhanskaia neft: poiski ravnodeistvuiushchey" in Furman, op. cit., 379-434; Heradstveit, D., "Democratic Development in Azerbaijan and the Role of Western Oil Industry," *Central Asian Survey,* 2001, 3, 261-88; Heradstveit, D., *Democracy and Oil: The Case of Azerbaijan,* Reichert, Wiesbaden, 2001.

host in 2020 or 2024, under the assumption that facilities would be improved to accommodate a massive influx of visitors.

Azerbaijan gradually came to be viewed as a petrostate, although this is somewhat inaccurate, since at least part of the economy exists outside of the oil industry. The boom has not been without its complexities, one of which has been known as the "resource curse," or "Dutch disease," and is a frequent consequence of hydrocarbon abundance. The term refers to the negative effects of improperly managed natural resources. It was originally coined to describe the aftermath of the 1960s discovery of natural gas deposits in a region of the North Sea owned by the Netherlands. There, the resources were extracted at low cost and in large quantities, thus squeezing out other exports. By itself, this is not a big problem, provided that the decline of production does not prevent the economy's overall long-term growth in the face of international competition.

Oil extraction by itself does not create many jobs, and the Dutch disease discourages large-scale, multifaceted industrialization. Unemployment has led to mass labor migration from the provinces to Baku, and, as the capital cannot provide the desired amount of employment, the migration has turned abroad, mainly to Russia. In fact, remittances from Russia have become an important source of national income, and the labor migration has in many ways built stronger ties than during the Soviet period.

Baku was changing at a rapid pace, even without the presence of the Bakintsi. With the post-Soviet revival of international interest in Caspian Sea oil resources, Baku firmly entered the second boom. Foreign and domestic investment funds initiated a great number of construction projects in and around the city, whose skyline was marked by newly built or nearly finished high-rise buildings, some even collapsing because of hasty work or earth tremors. These feverish and inevitably chaotic construction activities did little to alleviate the city's refugee housing problems, since real estate prices skyrocketed.

The growth of the city overwhelmed municipal services, especially the water supply, but also electricity and gas. The massive increase in car ownership has also outpaced the city's maintenance of its streets, not to mention its ability to train residents to drive properly. Baku still presents a sharp contrast between the oasis of prosperity and luxury that is its center and the impoverished outskirts and provinces.

A new entrepreneurial class has also begun to emerge with the second boom, and, through growing contacts with Western Europe and America, the educated post-Soviet groups are acquiring their own outlook of a cosmopolitan stratum. Use of the English language has been a rapidly growing feature of these groups, in business and in education, most notably as the language of instruction at private universities, and it challenges the position held by Russian.

Nevertheless, what truly sets the two booms apart is that during the first boom, Baku grew into a thoroughly multiethnic and multicultural urban center, a world unto itself and vastly different from the rest of Azerbaijan. But in the current boom, the city is a community of native Azeris, no longer separate, but an integral part of Azerbaijan. The population exchange, a step favored for a long time by neutral observers as a measure for reducing tensions between the ethnic communities, has been carried out—at a high cost to many. The results are likely to be irreversible, except for the return of refugees from Azerbaijan to the regions occupied by the Armenians. Mutual massacres of the urban population on the scale of January 1990 or of earlier years—1918 and 1905-1907—have poisoned the collective memories of generations and cannot repeat themselves. Moreover, South Caucasus has entered a phase of a new oil-based prosperity, and in the past such periods have been free of ethnic violence. If lessons from history are valid, it is not out of the question that the present boom, instead of prolonging the present conflict, might function as an inducement for its end and for the creation of new ties reinforcing a sense of regional unity and security.

Villages of Balakhan and Ribunchi near Baku, 1888.

In the words of the author of the most comprehensive study of post-Soviet Azerbaijan, the crux of many social issues that confront the country is whether, in the long run, the state embraces or ignores the rural population. "Given the size of Baku and its economic activity compared to the rest of the country, the risk that Baku would effectively swallow Azerbaijan could not be ignored. Bridging the gap between the city and the rest of the country will be a key challenge in the country's development."[26]

26. Cornell, S., *Azerbaijan since Independence,* New York, 2011, 428.

Martyrs of Islam, Tatars after the Schachsei-Wachsei Festival.

Tatars in the Mosque.

Бакинская арба.   Кавказскіе Типы.
Type d'une voiture, employée par les tartares à Bacou.   Types de Caucase

A type of vehicle owned by a Tatar in Baku.

A. P. Bogolyubov, *Baku*, 1861
Ink, brush, pencil, and paper.

Baku Culture

JAHANGIR SELIMKHANOV
& FARAH ALIYEVA

———————
———————

FOLLOWING THE SUDDEN LIFTING of the Iron Curtain, Azerbaijanis could finally enjoy the long-denied freedom to communicate with the outside world. Prior to 1990, when Azerbaijanis traveled abroad, simply explaining where they came from could be a challenging task. At best, someone might recall through deep layers of memory, "Yes, yes, Baku, of course, oil!" However, when meeting fellow musicians, Azerbaijanis often proudly discovered that Baku did occupy a place in the imagination thanks to its cultural heritage. Baku was the birthplace of Mstislav Rostropovich, the great cellist. Baku inspired a beautiful folk song arranged by Luciano Berio that has been a staple in the repertoire of contemporary music ensembles worldwide. Baku was also the performance backdrop for Arseni Avraamov's *Symphony of Sirens,* a remarkably bold sound experiment that was influential in the history of twentieth-century music and was justly considered a precursor of the *musique concrète* movement.

Baku's culturescape has indeed experienced a progression from happy coincidence to mutual curiosity and then on to interaction and hybrid cultural expressions. Proof of this is seen in Baku's music, theater, and film of this period. They are presented throughout this essay in a kaleidoscopic spontaneity rather than as an attempt to convey a comprehensive study or firmly substantiated interpretation of Bakuvian culture.

Baku's impressive cultural legacy is not widely known, and the examples above may provide readers with useful context. Each of them sprung from the happy "alchemical reaction" that occurred when a fin de siècle oil boom indirectly led to Baku's emergence as an open, cosmopolitan, striving, vibrant city with a rich cultural life. Of course, there were more complex causes for Baku's blossoming than simply the explosion of oil wealth or the influx of adventurous people from lands near and far, but ultimately the "black gold" generated intangible but valuable cultural capital.

It is instructive, if somewhat symbolic, to note that Leopold Rostropovich was one of those outstanding music professors from Moscow and Saint Petersburg who was invited to teach at the Baku conservatory during the oil boom in the 1920s. In his youth, Rostropovich took lessons from the legendary master cellist Pablo Casals in Paris. (It is remarkable that Baku cello students were enjoying training of such a high caliber.) Many years later, his son, Mstislav, who was born while the family lived in Baku, became so acclaimed throughout the world that the International Cello Competition in Paris was named in his honor. It is gratifying for Bakintsi to visit the Arsenal, a superb concert hall in Metz, France, and see a memorial star embossed into the floor at the entrance stating that their fellow Bakuvian countryman, Maestro Rostropovich, had inaugurated the opening of the hall. Baku is made even prouder by the fact that not only did that great musician happen by chance to be born in Baku but he also frequently stated that the city had an inexplicable cultural magnetism as well as a uniquely sensitive and understanding

Kerosene vendors.

audience. This inspired a new cultural brand for Baku; the city has celebrated the International Rostropovich Music Festival annually since 2007.

As mentioned above, another of Baku's claims to fame is a song in the "Folk Songs" cycle that Italian composer Luciano Berio arranged for his wife, the American singer Cathy Berberian. The singer was unaware of the specific origin of the song, which she had heard on an old gramophone record left by her father, which explains why the piece was simply titled "Azerbaijan Love Song," and why the text in the score is not rendered exactly, since it was done by ear from the record. Berio's "Azerbaijan Love Song" turns out to be the Azerbaijani folk song "Bu gün ayın üçüdür" (Today is the third day of the month), which is especially well known in Azerbaijan thanks to the legendary Rashid Beybutov's recording from the 1950s.

The surprisingly wide international circulation of records containing Azerbaijani music is a reminder that foreign record companies actively produced records with Azerbaijani traditional and folk music starting in the early 1900s. The very first company to enter the market was Gramophone, a British label. Gramophone was followed by French, Polish, and Russian competitors.

Long before the advent of globalization, the invention of "world music," and other efforts to nurture in Western listeners the habit of exploring exotic musical cultures, the Mugam Trio,[1] led by the famous singer Meshadi Muhammad Farzaliyev, toured Europe from 1923 to 1925. They performed successfully in Berlin, Vienna, Budapest, Bucharest, Paris, Brussels, and London. Evidently, this tour took them a couple of years, not only due to the slower modes of transportation then available but also because the group played several concerts in each city.

The third musical achievement mentioned above was the *Symphony of Sirens*. A studio reconstruction of the original score has recently been released by a British label, ReR, thanks to the efforts of a Spanish team of electroacoustic music specialists led by Miguel Molina Alarcon. The CD release notes described *Symphony of Sirens* as a "public sound event originally conceived in 1922, consisting of factory sirens, military regiments, steam locomotives, and choirs, all representing

1. *Mugam* is a form of Azerbaijani traditional music that is based on an elaborate system of modal scales. It requires refined professional performance skills and devoted listening skills.

Built with certain Japanese influence,
later the Baku Worker Theater, and now
the Russian Drama Theater.

the lively sonic signature of the port city of Baku."[2] The question immediately arises: "Why Baku?" This is not an easy question to answer, but there are several possibilities. For one, all through the oil boom and into the early Soviet period, Baku was often used as a testing ground for innovations and new technologies on behalf of the entire Soviet Union—and not just in oil extraction. Baku-Sabunchi-Surakhany was the first electric train in the Soviet Union, and the functional geometrical forms of constructivist landmarks and experimental housing blocks of the late 1920s and early 1930s illustrate that Baku was at the forefront of early Soviet architecture as well. An alternate explanation is that in the period after the Russian Revolution, Baku became a home for a number of exiled Russian "Silver Age" poets, including symbolists, futurists, and acmeists. Significant literary figures of this period, such as Sergei Gorodetsky, Alexei Kruchyonykh, Velimir Khlebnikov, and Vladimir Mayakovsky, visited Baku or lived there. Vyacheslav Ivanov lectured at Baku University from 1921 to 1924 and earned his doctorate there for his research on the Dionysian cult in Ancient Greece. These small details, often seemingly unrelated to the described event, help to reconstruct the context of Baku at this time and breathe life into piles of otherwise senseless historical information.

2. *Baku: Symphony of Sirens—Sound Experiments in the Soviet Avant Garde.* Original documents and recon http://www.rermegacorp.com/Merchant2/merchant.mv?.

It is a common view that, while digging into the facts of the past, we necessarily have in mind some "constructed" picture that we wish to make clearer, or an idea we hope to prove, to reinforce our personal beliefs and behaviors. Maybe we are driven to find a source of pride or to gain insight into the future. Otherwise, dealing with history would not be such an intriguing and exciting exercise. Why are we trying to collect, safeguard, and reconstruct these disappearing memories of old Baku? No doubt, there is a layer of subjectivity in one's cultural identity, and it is especially interesting for those who were born and raised in this city. However, it is surely also because we believe that Baku between the 1900s and 1920s was a great experiment in multiculturalism, cultural tolerance and convergence, intercultural dialogue, cultural colonialism, and postcolonialism—those notions that are currently occupying the minds of experts in charge of cultural policy, research, and practice.

Relations between cultures and subcultures are subject to analysis, theoretical reflection, and attempts to guide and "engineer," supported by intensive channels of electronic "second reality." However, in Old Baku it happened in a seemingly natural way. Were there cultural clashes within the narrow territory of this rapidly growing and developing city? How smooth was the process of reconciling "foreign" music cultures with the thriving indigenous and local music traditions that had arisen earlier? Did the cultivation of European theater, music, and entertainment forms in a Muslim country serve as a symbolic sign of prestige and power? We are not able to address these serious questions here, but we may conclude that Baku's situation differed in a positive way from that of many other cities around the world that were destined to multiculturalism.

Apparently, ethnic minorities in Baku felt free to nurture and express their national cultures. In the Baku newspapers of the period, we find ads and reports regarding intensive activity by Georgian, Armenian, Jewish, Ukrainian, Iranian, Polish, Latvian, Tatar, and German cultural societies. These cultural societies were quite different from the self-defensive and self-protective attitudes of immigrant cultures in contemporary multicultural megalopolises. And there is no evidence of the opposite extreme, in which elements of the invaders' cultures are forcefully imposed onto a "first nation" (as in the case of Bolivian baroque music, which was imposed by Spanish missionaries).

Evidently, European culture was first brought to Baku by "newcomers" for "internal circulation," and divided the cultural life into barely intersecting circles. However, it seems that cultural segregation was not really as dramatic or painful as is often presumed. The musical comedy *Arshin Mal Alan*, Uzeyir (Hajibeyli) Hajibeyov's 1913 masterpiece, is a symbolic embodiment of Baku's culture of that period. The stage design features eclectic interior decoration, including Eastern rugs and swords hanging on the walls, along with a gramophone and Marie Antoinette crystal chandeliers. The costumes harmoniously combine a national

Astrakhan hat with a European frock coat and, of course, the music merges Azerbaijani folk tunes with Italian aria. Bakintsi, especially the local youth of the 1900s, nurtured multilayered cultural identities. Many educated young men and women of that period were well acquainted with Persian poetry, on one hand, and had started to acquire Russian, German, and French books, on the other. Today, when we see hundreds (and at some festivals, even thousands) of classical music fans at symphonic concerts and opera performances in Baku, the audience is mostly local. The few expatriates within the crowd are an exception. In this case, the prevalence of Bakuvian attendees is not due to random fluctuations in cultural preferences by different audience groups. Indeed, classical music's popularity with Azerbaijanis is rooted in Baku's uninterrupted, generations-long process of cultivating interest in European classical music.

As has happened many times in the history of art, lack of stylistic purity, eclecticism and hybridity, and rule breaking—whether intentional or out of ignorance—led to new styles and forms of art. The naïve, bizarre, and bold idea of a twenty-three-year-old schoolteacher to create an opera from pieces of the centuries-old traditional *mugam* repertoire and some fragments written by a young visionary became *Leyli and Majnun,* a *mugam* opera staged in Baku in 1908 to critical acclaim. The audience was so excited by the news of this new form of musical entertainment that the performance sold out well in advance. As the newspapers reported, there were also many Westerners curious to see a quirky Oriental "opera," and people traveled all the way from Iran and Turkey to attend. This was the first attempt in the Islamic world to compose an opera. Retrospectively, we can acknowledge that the opera didn't lead to the development of other Western music compositions in the region—except perhaps in Azerbaijan. Azerbaijani music of the last hundred years should not be measured by achievements and benchmarks (in the postmodern era, we strongly believe that the idea of progress is not applicable to the history of culture). Azerbaijan's contemporary music scene has apparently maintained its distinctive voice but is no longer current with music composition worldwide.

However, let us return to times past. Any city with a lengthy history maintains in its collective memory a repertoire of favorite anecdotes and legends that are familiar to its citizens and eagerly told to outsiders. In Baku, one such story is related to the construction of the Opera House. The Russian singer Antonina Nezhdanova, whom opera historians and critics consider one of the finest sopranos of the twentieth century, is associated in Baku not only with a beloved melody (Rachmaninoff's "Vocalise" is dedicated to her) but also with the initiative to build a permanent venue for opera performances in Baku (though this may be a vernacular legend). The singer's tour in Baku was a sensation. She gave concerts at the Winter Club, the Baku Stock Exchange, and even the wooden circus. At the farewell dinner held at the casino in her honor, the singer was asked, "Madame, when will you bless Bakintsi with your visit once again?" The prima donna resolutely answered, "Perhaps never again. I'm not accustomed to singing in a casino or a circus! I wonder, why is there no opera theater in your beautiful and rich city, where so many generous people are living?" One of the local millionaires, Daniel Mailov, immediately promised the famous singer that as soon as she returned from a yearlong tour in Japan, a new opera house would be ready for inauguration in Baku.

Another story not proven by documents is that Mailov made a bet with Zeynalabdin Taghiyev, the famous patron and leading figure in philanthropic, educational, and cultural sponsorship in Baku, who believed that it was not possible to erect an eight-hundred-seat building with sophisticated acoustic requirements and elaborate interior decor in that time. The terms were as follows: If Mailov kept his promise, Taghiyev would compensate him for all expenses. Otherwise, Mailov would have to hand the opera house over to Taghiyev as soon as construction was finished. Unbelievably, the venue was ready within ten months. Nevertheless, take aside romantic details—from April 1910 to February 1911, construction was carried out twenty-four hours a day, in three shifts that simultaneously engaged two hundred workers. At night, the construction site was illuminated with spotlights. Nezhdanova immediately received a telegram inviting her to attend the opening of the new Opera House. Incidentally, the next year, she had a triumphant appearance in Paris, sharing the stage with such great counterparts as Enrico Caruso and Titta Ruffo.

Touring opera collectives regularly visited Baku from the late 1890s on, and after a permanent opera company was established in Baku, there has been no shortage of expatriate singers. Baku opera enthusiasts remember the rise of local opera stars whose names were accompanied by fame and adoration. The path to recognition was not easy for many of them, especially for Azerbaijani women. In the early years of national music theater, female roles were played by male actors, as it would have been quite risky to experiment with established moral conventions by allowing an Azerbaijani woman to appear onstage and sing.

The first singer who bravely decided to take this step was Shovket Mamedova. Born and raised in Tiflis, Shovket came to Baku to seek support to study as an opera singer in Milan. Zeynalabdin Taghiyev generously agreed to provide a scholarship for the young singer, and she started her lessons with Dotti Ambrosio. However, after less than a year, Taghiyev suddenly withdrew his subsidy (probably due to the fact that local society condemned his support of an Azerbaijani girl appearing onstage). In 1912 Uzeyir Hajibeyov, Huseyngulu Sarabski, Hanafi Teregulov, and other leading figures of Baku's musical theater decided to assist the young singer in getting a reputable professional education, and they arranged an income for Mamedova from the performance of the musical comedy *ər və arvad* (Husband and wife) to fund her studies in Italy. After the performance, the organizers announced that the young singer would appear for the first time onstage. This was a surprise for much of the audience, and although Shovket's singing was not interrupted, her friends found it necessary to carry her away immediately after the event and take her to a secret safe place. Soon after, they transported her to Tiflis. She returned to Baku only after nine years, and a few years later she realized her dream to visit Italy. Mamedova spent two years in Italy (1927-29), but this time in a different capacity—as an already mature, confident, acknowledged master.

Leafing through the old Baku newspapers is inspiring and instructive for a music historian. There are so many facts, and so many familiar and unfamiliar names that surprise and puzzle one. For instance, Baku was introduced to a rare, authentic approach toward early music performance by the harpsichordist Wanda Landowska, experiments by American protagonist of modern dance Isadora Duncan, nightingale coloraturas by the world-class Finnish opera singer Alma Fohstrøm, the thundering bass of the legendary Fyodor Chaliapin, sacred organ music sessions in the city's Lutheran church, Krakow wedding scenes, the unique sound of the Ševčík Quartet (three of the ensemble's four members—Bohuslav Lhatsky, Karel Procházka, and Karel Moravec—were pupils of the famous Czech violin teacher Otakar Ševčík), bel canto by touring Italian opera casts (an Internet search reveals that a seventy-eight-inch disc by tenor Alessandro Scalabrini is on sale through a Buenos Aires-based rare records dealer, and his photo is kept in the collection at the University of Washington), and the delicate and complex language of Japanese theater traditions presented by Ganako Oota and her company.

In 1902 the very first "Eastern concert" took place in Baku in the Taghiyev Theater. The theater had established the tradition of performing Azerbaijani traditional music in a concert hall, with all of the appropriate elements of Western practice, including public attendance, ticket sales, a division between the stage and audience seats, promotion through posters and newspapers, and so on. In a review after the historic Eastern concert, a critic noted that all of the tickets had sold out and that the audience had been quite diverse, so one can deduce that many people from different ethnic origins attended this unusual concert.

The audience for opera was also steadily growing in Baku, and it became a favorite cultural attraction for our grandparents' generation, along with dramatic theater, which had much older traditions in Azerbaijan. The list of operas that were presented in Baku in the first decades of the twentieth century contains not only omnipresent favorites such as *La Traviata, Aida,* and *Carmen,* but also such pieces as *La Juive* by Fromental Halévy, *Zazà* by Ruggero Leoncavallo, *L'Africaine* by Giacomo Meyerbeer, and *Mignon* by Ambroise Thomas. Curiously enough, Jules Massenet is represented in this list by at least three operas—*Werther, Thaïs,* and *Le portrait de Manon*—all just a few years after they were first composed and staged.

The ideals of national enlightenment that were championed by Miza Fathali Akhundzada and Hasanbey Zardabi, and further developed by a plethora of outstanding writers, journalists, and educators have been reflected in the cathartic role of the drama in the life of Baku society. National plays were attended by audiences with special enthusiasm, although some foreign masterpieces, such as Shakespeare's *Othello* and Schiller's *Die Räuber,* became "must-sees" for generations of theatergoers in Baku.

Huseyn Arablinski was a great actor on the Azerbaijani theatrical stage. Despite his modest personal character, his performances sparked a cult of admirers, and tickets to plays in which he performed usually sold out a week in advance. Throughout his short life, Arablinski was surrounded by the attention and adoration of women. For instance, his name came from a moment in which he was moved by a romantic impulse and decided to take the artistic pseudonym Arablinski in the memory of a beautiful young girl. She had attended all of his performances when his company toured in Makhachkala, a town in Dagestan. He could not marry her because he was just a poor actor, and she was the daughter of General Arablinski. Another time, Arablinski became a victim of the attentions of an influential but married woman. After she lost hope of enticing him, she hired a murderer to take the life of Baku's beloved actor—much like the plot of a theatrical tragedy.

Many of the forms, concepts, and habits of Western culture translated quite smoothly to Baku, and perhaps only the visual arts were somewhat delayed. This may have been a result of the centuries-long aversion to "imitating nature," but the traditions of visual art in the Western sense were almost completely absent in Baku. There was the inspiring example of Qajar painting, a short-lived trend that circulated quite narrowly in Iran (but was indispensable to the art history of Azerbaijan), which combined in a fresh and bold way the elements of Safavid book miniatures with Western portraiture. Of course, as with many other artistic forms, the first stage of acquaintance with Western art came through "imported" examples, and gradually local youth became involved in the process of revisiting and reproducing the unfamiliar "languages" of this art.

Local satiric periodicals provided a great service in the appropriation by mass viewers of pictorial visual culture in Azerbaijan. It was an internationally shared habit of this period to laugh about serious issues, including politics, social inequality, common stereotypes, and so on via cabaret culture, vaudevilles, and satirical magazines. In Baku, in a short period between 1906 and 1913, such magazines appeared and disappeared rather quickly. They included "Bəhlul," "Zənbur," "Mirat," "Arı," "Kəlniyyət," and others, although one should not omit *Molla Nəsrəddin*, which even lasted into the Soviet period and was published for another twenty-four years. Interestingly, German illustrators Oskar Schmerling, Josef Rotter, and Benedict Tellingater contributed to these publications, where the trendy-looking European graphic styles and printing techniques of the period combined with local Bakuvian faces and costumes, and with unusually fresh-looking Arabic script. Along with these experienced and well-trained artists

(Schmerling, for example, was a graduate of the famous Akademie der Schöner Künste in Munich), the young self-taught cartoonist-illustrator Azim Azimzade worked on *Molla Nəsrəddin*. His graphic sketches of Baku's typical characters are full of vivacity and humor. It is a curious fact that the legacy of *Molla Nəsrəddin* still remains one hundred years later. Very recently, a new publication of selected caricatures from this magazine was arranged by the famous artist collective Slavs and Tatars.

It didn't take long, though, for Baku to start nurturing visual arts professionals. In 1920 the State Art College was established in Baku. Since the early 1930s, there has been an outburst of talented painters, sculptors, and graphic artists. An instructive anecdote from recent times proves that the traditions of classical drawing and sculpture have been well taught in Baku for decades. In the late 1990s three young sculptors from Baku participated in an international competition for jobs at Madame Tussaud's Studios in London. To general surprise, when the results of the blind selection held in New York were disclosed, it turned out that all three positions were awarded to fellow graduates of Baku's art school. But the Baku artists' acquisition of classical techniques and aesthetic norms was paralleled by their absorption of up-to-date visual impulses. A glimpse of *At the Spinning Factory,* a picture dated 1930, by young Salam Salamzadeh, reveals the pure energy, sincere naïveté, and spirit of novelty that was characteristic of progressive art trends of the time.

The youngest of the arts, cinema, was quickly established in Baku. It took just three years from the first public showing of the cinematograph—the invention of Auguste and Louis Lumière—for the cinema to arrive in Baku. A few short moving pictures shot in Baku for the World's Fair were presented in 1898. One of them featured an oil field fire in Balakhany, a Baku suburb. It took eighteen more years for Baku to start making feature films and get put on the map of film-producing locations. Unsurprisingly, the very first feature film in Azerbaijani history relates to oil, the dominant theme in and around Baku. The film was titled *In the Kingdom of Oil and Millions.* It also came as no surprise that the cast of main characters included leading theater actor Huseyn Arablinski. In a scene that takes place at a wedding party, the roles of the musicians are "played" by legendary *mugam* musicians, including singer Jabbar Garyagdy and *tar* player Gurban Pirimov. Documentary research reveals that there were five cinemas in Baku in 1910, and by 1915 that number had grown to eight.

Film viewing was just one of many available forms of popular culture and entertainment. Music critic and journalist Fariza Babayeva reviewed ads in the local newspapers of the period for the first evidence of jazz in Baku, and he argues that there were no fewer than ten performance venues in 1907 in a town with 150,000 inhabitants—the Opera House, the Taghiyev Theater, the circus of the Nikitin brothers, the vaudeville Palais de Cristal theater, the hall at the Grand Hotel, and

The Minaret, 1905.

HUSEYN ARABLINSKI

many more. A 1907 advertisement for the Gramophone Stock Corporation states that their record offerings included 20,000 titles in seventy languages. A 1922 poster illustrates the arrival of exotic music from overseas. The public was invited to attend a "negro sketch" by the title "Black Betsy" in the "Chat Savage" theater. Baku's cosmopolitan young crowds were eager to dance to this trendy music from the early 1920s on, only a few years after the arrival of newborn jazz. This jazz craze was not warmly welcomed by the Stalinist ideological machine, and in some periods was quite dangerous to pursue, but already starting in the 1930s Baku had firmly established itself as a true jazz city, at least by the standards of the vast Soviet empire. Unfortunately, those practicing and appreciating jazz were soon isolated from kindred spirits by the Iron Curtain, but this is another story, for a different book.

We hope this brief overview has conveyed a hint of the city's unique, open, cosmopolitan, and culture-addicted flair, so that in the future it will be easier to find the right answer to the surprised question: "Why Baku?"

Vasily Vasilyevich Vereshchagin
Baku View from the Sea, 1872
Oil on canvas, 50 × 99.5 cm

Городской Садъ и гавань. Баку.
Jardin de ville et la baie. Bakou.

The city garden and the bay.

Old Baku's Cinematography Traditions

FUAD AKHUNDOV

THE CINEMATOGRAPHIC HISTORY of pre-Soviet Baku to a great extent takes after the city's turbulent oil history, and is closely related to it—in fact, it is as old as the history of cinematography itself. Baku's first local film, *Oil Wells of Baku: Close View,* was shot as early as 1896, only a year after the camera was invented by brothers Auguste and Louis Lumière. The name of the film speaks for itself and, according to some cinema historians, such as Bertrand Tavernier, "may be the first ecological film ever made."[1]

A thirty-six-second segment (now available on YouTube) was shot by Kamil Serf with a stationery camera. The film depicts huge flames streaming from a burning oil well, not an unusual event in old Baku. From today's vantage point, this looks like an environmental disaster, however, in the film it looks more like a spectacle. Even though the camera never moves throughout the visual narrative, the vibrant image it captures—the magnificence of fire—captivates viewers.[2]

It is no surprise that, with the rapid development of Baku at the time of the invention of the cinématographe, the city became one of the major regional hubs of this new art form. Another Russian of French descent, Alexander Mishon, a professional photographer and cameraman, practiced his trade in Baku for twenty-five years, from roughly 1879 until 1908. Mishon established the city's most prestigious studio on Mikhailovsky Street, one of downtown's liveliest streets.

Not only did Mishon leave an invaluable legacy of photographs of Baku and the oil fields, he also established a scientific photo club and, only two years after Kamil Serf's work, succeeded in shooting motion pictures. The first films shot by Mishon depicted short scenes from the city's daily life, such *The Festivity in the City Park, Train Entering the Railway Station, Departure of a Steamer of the Caucasus & Mercury Shipping Company,* and *The Market Street Early in the Morning.*

1. Tavernier, *Lumiere Brothers' First Films.*
2. *Ecology and Spectacle,* 19-20.

БАКУ. Меркурьевскаъ улица
BACOU. Rue Mercourievskaia

Merkurievskaya street.

The trailers were first presented on June 21, 1898. Only a month later, the following announcement was made by *Kaspi*, the popular local daily:

On Sunday, August 2, 1898, A. Mishon will show some motion pictures that he has taken with a Lumière movie camera and which has been improved by the engineer Jules Carpentier. These films of the Caucasus and Central Asia have been prepared for the forthcoming International Paris Exhibition and will be presented only once in Baku at the V. I. Vasilyev-Vyatski Circus Theater.

The following films will be shown: *Fire Resulting from an Oil Gusher at Bibi-Heybat Oil Field, The Departure Ceremony of His Excellency Amir of Bukhara by the Grand Duke Alexei Steamship, A Folk Dance of the Caucasus,* and scenes from the comedy *Caught Red-handed* ("Popalsya"), which was presented recently at one of Baku's parks. For more details see the posters. Starts at 21:00.[3]

Mishon repeated the presentation on August 5, 1898, replacing the two later pieces with life scenery from Balakhany, one of Baku's oil-rich suburbs. No doubt the event was a sensational success, and a hundred-plus years later, in 2000, August 2 was officially recognized as Cinema Day in Azerbaijan.

The first Baku films were very successful at the famous Paris Exhibition of 1900, attracting a number of foreigners to the oil-booming city. Interestingly enough, some of Mishon's footage still exists. His *Folk Dance in the Caucasus* was later used in a documentary, and scenes from *Oil Gush Fire in Bibi-Heybat* were shown in 1995 in France, at the commemoration ceremony of world cinema's one hundredth anniversary.

In 1899 Hassan-bey Zardabi, a renowned local journalist and public figure, noted the following: "Now we have in our hands a toy machine called 'cinematographe.' This wonderful machine was produced only a short time ago and looks just a toy. You can find this machine which is called 'stroboscope' in many optician's shops."[4]

3. *Kaspi,* August 1, 1898.
4. *Kaspi,* November 27, 1898.

In 1906 Baku-based cameraman and projectionist Vasily Amashukeli started
filming various scenes of the city's day-to-day life. This resulted in trailers such as
*Baku's Bazaar Characters, Stone and Coal Transportation, Seaside Walk, Work at
the Oil Fields, Oil Extraction* (1907). Other works, filmed with cameraman Mikhail
Grossman in 1908, include *The Black and White Towns, Balakhany,* and *Nobel
Enterprises.* In later decades Amashukeli became one of the founding fathers of
Georgian cinema.

The Pirone brothers from Belgium were among the major cinema producers
of pre-Soviet Baku. Their studio, Filma, was established in 1915. It was the Pirones
who invited Boris Svetlov, a filmmaker and director from Saint Petersburg, to Baku
to produce some extraordinary pieces, such as *The Kingdom of Oil and Millions.*
The film was shown on May 14, 1916, at the Taghiyev Mall. However, since it was
a full-length film, it was also shown in successive parts on May 14 and 27. The
movie features Husseyn Arablinski, the famous Azeri actor; Gurban Primov, a
well-known performer of *mugam,* the traditional Azeri music; and a renowned
dancer, Madatov.

Another work by Svetlov was *Cloth Peddler (Arhin mal alan),* based on Uzeyir
Hajibeyov's famous operetta of the same name. However, the film's poor sound
quality forced the composer to insist upon suspending further showings at local
cinemas. Other works by Svetlov included *The Woman, An Hour before His Death,*
and *An Old Story in a New Manner.*

The revolutionary year 1917 presented Baku with some interesting newsreel
footage that passed along the message of the turbulent public events unfolding
in the aftermath of the Russian Empire's collapse. The names of the reels speak

Outside of the cinema.

for themselves: *The Freedom Festivities in Baku on March 12, 1917; March 1917 and the Struggle for the Labor Contract; Speech by a Baku Commissar at a Meeting;* and *Oil Drilling and Extraction.* Fragments of the two latter works are still cherished in the Azerbaijan National Archives of Photo and Cinema Documents.

The first Republic of Azerbaijan (1918–20) had ambitious plans for the national cinema. The footage of that period consists mainly of patriotic newsreels and documentaries. A chronicle depicting the ceremony celebrating the Republic's first anniversary in 1919 was broadly shown in Baku's major movie theaters, such as *Express, Record, and Forum.* However, the first Republic of Azerbaijan was short-lived, so its prospects regarding the national cinema remained unimplemented.

Baku's takeover by Communists troops in April 1920 opened a new era in the local cinema history. Soviet authorities, fully understanding the role of cinema as the most efficient tool for managing the masses, were very serious in their approach to this most popular art form, viewing it as "the only means of propaganda not requiring any background and particularly suitable for the Oriental masses with their inclination to images as opposed to logical reasoning."[5]

It was the Soviet authorities of Azerbaijan who established the first Cinema Factory in 1922 by nationalizing the Pirone brothers' Filma. A year later, the Azerbaijan Photo Film Institution was incorporated pursuant to the decree of the Council of People's Commissars.[6] The Renaissance restaurant, with adjacent facilities, was adapted to accommodate the newly established Cinema Factory.

The new facility was soon equipped with cutting-edge US equipment, facilities for film development, utilities, and a sizable movie theater.[7] Headed by Khanafi Teregulov, a gifted local opera performer and public figure, and Muslim Magomayev, a renowned composer and grandfather of the iconic performer Muslim Magomayev, the Cinema Factory proved to be very efficient, with *The Maiden Tower* cinema novel as one of its first brilliant works. That being said, for the following seven decades, the cinema became a state-owned ideological tool.

5. *Novy Vostok,* 1925, 9.
6. *Bakinski Rabochi,* August 29, 1923.
7. Ibid.

PINKHOS SABSAY
An outstanding Baku
sculptor from Odessa.

STATUE OF SERGEI KIROV
Made by P. Sabsay in the
German church of Baku
(a statue that saved the
church).

Celebration of Epiphany,
January 6, 1904.

Крещеніе 6-го Янв. 1904 на Парапетѣ.   Баку.
Fête des Rois le 6 Janvier 1904.   Bacou.

Изданіе I. П. Гуревича, Баку.

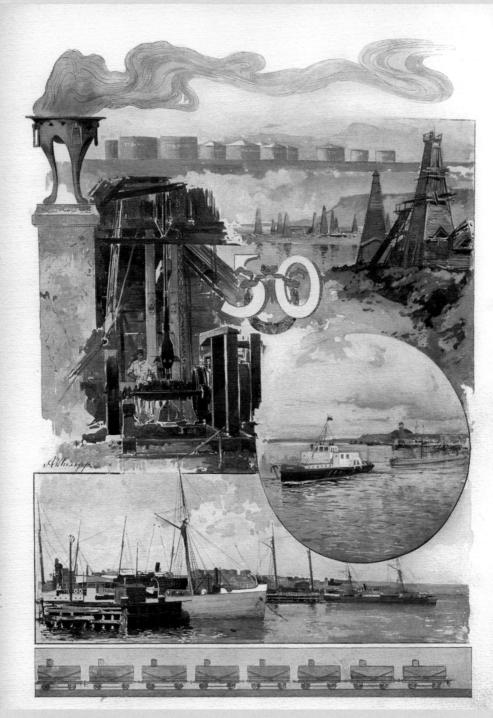

Leaf from the album "In Memory of the Fiftieth Anniversary
of Immanuel Ludvigovich Nobel, June 10, 1909."

Bibliography

Alakbarov, Farid. "The Memoirs of Actor Sarabski." *Azerbaijan International Magazine* 10, no. 3 (2002): 46-50.

Alakbarov, Farid. "Baku's Old City: Memories of About How It Used to Be." *Azerbaijan International Magazine* 10, no. 3 (2002): 38-45.

Alstadt, Audrey L. "The Azerbaijani Bourgeoisie and the Cultural-Enlightenment Movement in Baku: First Steps Towards Nationalism." In *Ronald Grigor Suny, ed., Transcaucasia, Nationalism and Social Change,* 199-209. Ann Arbor: University of Michigan Press, 1983, 1996.

Altstadt, Audrey L. *The Azerbaijani Turks: Power and Identity Under Russian Rule.* Stanford: Hoover Institution Press, 1992.

Baldauf, Ingeborg. *Schriftreform und Schriftwechsel bei den Muslimischen Russland und Sowjetturken (1850-1937).* Budapest: Kiado, 1993.

Baldauf, Ingeborg. *Writing Reform and Correspondence with the Muslim Russia and Soviet Turks (1850-1937).* Budapest: Kiado, 1993.

Blair, Betty. "Alphabet and Language in Transition." Special issue. *Azerbaijan International* 8, no.1 (Spring 2000): 33.

Dragadze, Tamara, ed. *Azerbaijan.* London: Melisende Fox Communications and Publications, 2000.

Farzaliyev, Chingiz. *Painting of Azerbaijan: Anthology.* Baku: Mega, 2007.

Hakluyt, R. *The Principal Navigations*, etc., vol. I, London, 1600.

Henry, James Dodds. *Baku: An Eventful History.* London: A. Constable & Co., 1905.

Heradstveit, Daniel. "Democratic Development in Azerbaijan and the Role of the Western Oil Industry," *Central Asian Survey*, vol. 20 (3) (2001): 261-88.

Heradstveit, Daniel. *Democracy and Oil: The Case of Azerbaijan.* Wiesbaden: Reichert, 2001.

Heydarov, Tale, and Taleh Bagiyev. *Azerbaijan: 100 Questions Answered.* London: Azerbaijani Society, 2006.

Heyerdahl, Thor. "Challenging Euro-Centric Theories of Migration." *Azerbaijan International Magazine* 3, no. 1 (1995): 60.

Ismailov, Eldar, and Vladimir Papava. *The Central Caucasus: Essays on Geopolitical Economy.* Luleå, Sweden: CA & CC Press, 2006.

Kaempfer, E. *Amoenitatum exoticarum politico-physico-medicarum fascisuli V.* Lemgo, 1712.

Landau, Jacob M., and Barbara Kellner-Heinkele. *Politics of Language in the Ex-Soviet Muslim States: Azerbaijan, Uzbekistan, Kazakhstan, Kyrgyzstan, Turkmenistan and Tajikistan.* Ann Arbor, MI: University of Michigan Press, 2001.

Liber, George. "Korenizatsia: Restructuring Soviet Nationality Policy in the 1920s." *Ethnic and Racial Studies* 14, no. 1 (1991): 15-23.

Marvin, Charles T. *The Region of the Eternal Fire: An Account of a Journey to the Petroleum Region of the Caspian in 1883.* London: W. H. Allen & Co., 1891.

Mirbabayev, Miryusif F. *Concise History of Azerbaijani Oil.* Baku: Azerneshr, 2007.

Monuments of Azerbaijan. Baku: Ministry of Culture and Tourism of the Azerbaijan Republik, 2007.

Murray, Robin L., and Joseph K. Heumann "Ecology and Spectacle in Oil Wells of Baku: Close View". In *Ecology and Popular Film: Cinema on the Edge.* Albany: State University of New York Press, 2009.

O'Lear, Shannon. "Azerbaijan's Resource Wealth: Political Legitimacy and Public Opinion." *Geographical Journal* 173, no. 3 (Sept. 2007): 207-23.

Qajar, Chingiz. *Old Baku.* Baku: OKA Ofset, 2009.

Rasizade, Alek. "Azerbaijan, the U.S., and Oil: Prospects on the Caspian Sea." *Journal of Third World Studies*, XVI, no. 1 (Spring 1991): 29-48.

Reiss, Tom. *The Orientalist.* New York: Random House, 2005.

Riddell, John. *To See the Dawn: Baku 1920—First Congress of the Peoples of the East.* New York: Pathfinder Press, 1993.

Said, Kurban. *Ali and Nino: A Love Story.* New York: Anchor, 2000.

Said, Kurban. *Girl from the Golden Horn.* New York: Overlook Press, 2001.

148 Salmanov, Emile, and Robert Chenciner. *Architecture of Baku: Fabled Capital of the Caspian.* Catalogue, March 7-April 20, 1985, Heinz Gallery. London: Royal Institute of British Architects, 1985.

Shaffer, Brenda. *Borders and Brethren: Iran and the Challenge of Azerbaijani Identity.* Suny, Ronald. *The Baku Commune, 1917-1918: Class and Nationality in the Russian Revolution.* Princeton: Princeton University Press, 1972.

Swietochowski, Tadeusz, and Brian C. Collins. *Historical Dictionary of Azerbaijan.* Lanham, MD: The Scarecrow Press, 1999.

Swietochowski, Tadeusz. *Russia and Azerbaijan: A Borderland in Transition.* New York: Columbia University Press, 1995.

Swietochowski, Tadeusz. *Russian Azerbaijan, 1905-1920: The Shaping of National Identity in a Muslim Community.* New York: Cambridge University Press, 1985.

Tolf, R. W. *The Russian Rockefellers: The Saga of the Nobel Family and the Russian Oil Industry.* Stanford: Stanford University Press, 1976.

Trevithick, F. H. *A Sketchy Report on the Petroleum Industry at Baku, May 1886.* Reprint of the edition published before 1923: Bibliolife, 2010, ISBN 1149727225, 9781149727225.

Villari, Luigi. *The Fire and Sword in the Caucasus.* London: T. F. Unwin Edition, 1906.

Voyages d'un Missionaire de la Compagnie de Jesus en Turkuie, en Perse, en Armenie, en Arabie, et en Barbarie. Paris, MDCCXX.

Yergin, Daniel. *Prize: The Epic Quest for Oil, Money and Power.* New York: Simon Shuster, 1991 / Cambridge: MA: MIT Press, 2002.

LITERATURE IN AZERBAIJANI

Bakıxanov, Abbasqulu ağa. *Gülüstani-İrəm.* Tərc. M. Əsgərli. Baku: Minarə, 2000 (in Azeri). Bakikhanov, Abbasqulu agha. *Paradise of Wisdom.* Translated by M. Asgarli. Baku: Minara, 2000.

Baykara, Hüseyn. *Azərbaycan istiqlal mübarizəsinin tarixi.* Bakı: Azərbaycan Dövlət Nəşriyyatı, 1992. Baykara, Hüseyn. *History of Struggle of Azerbaijan for Independence.* Baku: Azerbaijan State Publishing House, 1992.

Düma, Aleksandr. *Qafqaz.* Bakı: Qafqaz Strateji Araşdırmalar İnstitutu, 2010. Dumas, Alexander. *Caucasus.* Baku: Caucasian Institute of Strategic Studies, 2010.

Rəsulzadə, Məmməd Əmin. *Çağdaş Azərbaycan Tarixi.* Bakı: Gənclik, 1991. Rasulzade, Mammad Amin. *Modern History of Azerbaijan.* Baku: Ganjlik, 1991.

Sarabski, Hüseynqulu. *Köhnə Bakı.* Bakı: Elmlər Akademiyasının Nəşriyyatı, 1958. Sarabski, Huseinqulu. *Old Baku.* Baku: Academy of Sciences Publishing House, 1958.

Sarabski, Hüseynqulu. *Köhnə Bakı.* Bakı: Elmlər Akademiyasının Nəşriyyatı, 1967. Sarabski, Huseinqulu. *Old Baku.* Baku: Academy of Sciences Publishing House, 1967.

Süleymanov, Manaf. *Eşitdiklərim, oxuduqlarım, gördüklərim.* Bakı: Azərnəşr, 1987. Süleymanov, Manaf. *Memories about Things, Which I Heard, Read or Saw.* Baku: Azerneshr, 1987.

Süleymanov, Manaf. *Neft Milyonçusu.* Bakı: Azərbaycan Nəşriyyatı, 1995. Suleymanov, Manaf. *The Oil Baron.* Baku: Azerbaijan Press, 1995.

LITERATURE IN RUSSIAN

Аваков, Р.М. и А.Лисов. Россия и Закавказье: реальное партнерство. Москва: Финанстатинформ, 2000. Avakov, R. M., and A. Lisov. *Russia and Transcaucasus: Real Partnership.* Moscow: Finanstatinform: 2000.

Ахундов, Давуд. Архитектура древнего и раннесредневекового Азербайджана. Баку: Азернеш, 1986. Akhundov, Davud. *Architecture of Ancient and Early-Medieval Azerbaijan.* Baku: Azerneshr, 1986.

Ашурбейли, Сара. История города Баку. Баку: Азернеш, 1992. Ashurbeyli, Sara. *History of Baku City.* Baku: Azerneshr, 1992.

Бадалов, Рахман. "Баку: город и страна." В книге: Азербайджан и Россия: общества и государства. Под ред. Д.Е. Фурмана. М.: Летний сад, 2001: 256-279. Badalov, Rahman. "Baku: City and Country." In *Azerbaijan and Russia: Societies and States*, edited by D. E. Furman, 256-79. M.: Letniy Sad, 2001:

Байкал, Мурат. Великий бакинец—отец индийской нефти—нефтяной король мира. Баку: Qanun, 1911. Baykal, Murat. *The Great Bakuvian—Father of Indian Oil—Oil King of the World.* Baku, Qanun, 2011.

Баку : исторические и достопримечательные места. / АН Азербайджанской ССР ; сост.: Д. Д. Гаджинский, П. А. Азизбекова ; ред. М. А. Казиев. М.: АН СССР, 1956. *Baku: Historical and Important Sites.* / Academy of Sciences of Azerbaijan SSR; compiled by D. D. Hajinski, P. A. Azizbeyova; ed. M. A. Kaziyev. Moscow: USSR Academy of Sciences Press, 1956.

Баку и его районъ 1914. Ежегодник. Адресная и справочная книга. Баку, 1914. *Baku and Its Environs 1914.* Annual Information Handbook. Baku, 1914.

Баку. Баку: Главная редакция Азербайджанской Советской Энциклопедии, 1990. Переиздание оригинала: Санкт-Петербург: Типография Колпинского, 1902. *Baku:* Head Editorial of the Azerbaijan Soviet Encyclopedia, 1990. Originally published in 1902 by Tip. A. E. Kolpinskago, Saint Petersburg.

Illustration Credits

Бретаницкий Л. С. Баку. Архитектурно-художественные памятники. Ленинград: Искусство, 1965. Фотографии выполнены И. А.Рубенчиком.Bretanitski,L. S.Baku.Architectiral-Artistic Monuments. Leningrad: Iskusstvo, 1965. Photos by I. A. Rubenchik.

Велиев, Сейран. Древний, древний Азербайджан. Баку: Гянджлик, 1973. Veliyev, Seyran. Ancient, Ancient Azerbaijan. Baku: Ganjlik, 1973.

Гасанли, Джамиль. «Национальный вопрос в Азербайджане: правда и вымысел (1956–1959 гг.)» Зеркало 6, no. 81 (2006): 33. Gassanly, Jamil. "National question in Azerbaijan: The Truth and Fiction (1956–1959)". Zerkalo 6, no. 81 (2006): 33.

Дадашев С., Усейнов М. Архитектурные памятники Баку. Баку: Изд. Академии архитектуры, 1946. Dadashev, S., and M. Usey-nov. Architectural Manuments of Baku. Baku: Academy of Architecture Press, 1946.

Джуварлы, Тогрул. «Азербайджанская нефть: Поиски равнодействующей». В кн. Азербайджан и Россия: общества и государства. Под ред. Д.Е. Фурмана. М.: Летний сад, 2001: 379-434. Juvarli, Togrul. "Azerbaijani Oil: Search of the Resultant.". In Azerbaijan and Russia: Societies and States, edited by D. E. Furman. M.: Letniy Sad, 2001: 379-434 .

Земцов, Илья. Партия или мафия? Разворованная республика. Париж: Les Editeurs Reunis, 1970. Zemtsov, Ilya. Party or Maphia? The Plundered Republic. Paris: Les Editeurs Reunis, 1970.

Ибрагимов, М. Предпринимательская деятельность Г. з. Тагиева. Баку: Elm, 1990 . İbrahimov, M. Business activities of H. Z. Taghi-yev. Baku: Elm, 1990.

Миграция и урбанизация в СНГ и Балтии в 90-е годы. Под ред. Ж.А.Зайончковской. Центр изучения проблем вынужденной миграции в СНГ. М., 1999. Zaionchkovskaia, Z., ed. Migration and Urbanization in SNG in 90s. Center for Study of Problems of Forced Migration in SNG. M., 1999.

Самедов, Васиф и Шарифов, Азад. «Нефтяной король из Баку». Эхо плюс, 2 февраля 2002 г. http://www.azerigallery.com/bio/taghiyev-e .html. Samadov, Vasif, and Azad Sharifov. "Oil King from Baku." Echo Plus, February 2, 2002 (in Russian). Available at http://www.azerigallery .com/bio/taghiyev-e.html.

Сеидов, Вюгар. Архивы бакинских нефтяных фирм: XIX—начало XX в. Москва: Изд-во Модест Колеров, 2009. Seyidov, Vugar. Archives of the Baku Oil Companies: (19th to Early 20th Centuries). Moscow: Modest Kolerov Press, 2009.

Сулейманов, Манаф. Дни минувшие. Перевод Э.Ахундовой. Баку: Азернешр, 1990. Suley-manov, Manaf. The Bygone Days. Translated from Russian by E. Akhundova. Baku: Azernashr, 1990.

Сумбатзаде А.С. Азербайджанцы—этногенез и формирование народа. Баку: Элм, 1990. Sumbatzadeh, A. S. Azerbaijanians—Ethnogenesis and Formation of the Nation. Baku: Elm, 1990.

Тагиев Ф. А. История города Баку в первой половине XIX века (1806–1859). Б., Элм, 1999. Taghiyev, F. A. History of Baku in the First Half of the 19th Century (1806–1859). Baku: Элм, 1999.

Усейнов, М и Л. Бретаницкий, А. Саламзаде. История архитектуры Азербайджана. Москва: «Госстройиздат», 1963. Useynov, M., L. Bretanitsky, and A. Salamzadeh. History of Architecture in Azerbaijan. Moscow: Gosstroyiz-dat, 1963.

Шаммазов А. М. История развития нефтегазовой промышленности. М., 1999. Sham-mazov, A. M. History of Development of Oil and Gas Industry. Moscow, 1999.

Websites

Azerbaijan International, 1996-2011, http://www.azer.com/

Azerbaijan Today, 2005-2011, http://www.today.az/

"Heydər Əliyev və Türkçülük" mövzusunda tədbir keçirilib. Azərbaycan Xəbərləri. Gün.az http://gun.az/latest/4571?page=5&page_ slug=social

Наш Баку. История Баку и бакинцев. http://www.ourbaku.com/index.php5/

National Library of Russia, St. Petersburg: 2, 7 bottom, 8 right, 10, 13, 16, 55 top, 57 top, 60, 74, 75, 83 ,92, 111, 116, 123, 128, 146.

Archive Fuad Akhundov, Baku: 23, 25, 27-49, 53, 143, 144, 145 top.

Archive Pavel V.Khoroshilov, Moscow: 20, 21, 68, 69, 84, 112, 113, 114, 115, 125.

Archive Jahangir Selimbakhov, Baku: 130, 131, 138 right.

The Azerbaijan State Museum of Art , Baku: 139.

Collection Elchin Sarafov, Moscow: 108.

The map of Baku is courtesy of Suad Garayeva, London.

All other postcards and stamps are from the archive of Nicolas V.Iljine, Frankfurt am Main.

Biographies

———

Born on April 21, 1968 in Baku, **FUAD AKHUNDOV** refers to himself as *an enthusiastic historian of yesteryear Baku*. A Bachelor in Oriental Studies from the State University of Baku (class 1992) and Master in Public Administration from Harvard (2001), he had been serving at the National Central Bureau of Interpol in Azerbaijan for good fourteen years and is actively involved in written, oral, and simultaneous translation involving English, Russian, and Azeri.

Meanwhile Fuad has been passionately engaged in studies of the nineteenth to twentieth centuries Baku history, architecture and personalia for more than twenty years so far. His research of family stories and close links with the National Archives of Photo and Cinema Documents resulted in an impressive folder of heritage photos, which he lavishly shares during his untraditional walking tours in old parts of Baku, series of articles in local media and abroad, and, finally, a TV project *Bakinskiye Tayni (The Mysteries of Baku)* at *Ictimai (Public TV) Channel* in Baku as of 2006.

Fuad's TV show was recognized as *"The Best Culture and Education Oriented Programs of the CIS"* in 2006 and was decorated with a number of national awards in Azerbaijan, including prestigious *Humay Prize*.

Despite his emigration to Canada in 2007, Fuad Akhundov could never tear himself apart from Baku's eventful past and present, so as a Toronto resident now, he still remains every inch a Bakuvian in spirit. His input into this book is a vivid proof of this enduring affection.

In his leisure time Fuad loves collecting model cars and figures (scale 1:43). He is also an impassioned distance swimmer in the Caspian, a unique landlocked sea he believes to be second to none.

DR. FARID ALAKBARLI (b. 1964) is the president of the Azerbaijan Association of Medical Historians, Director of the Department of Information and Translation of the Institute of Manuscripts of the Azerbaijan National Academy of Sciences, Doctor of Historical Sciences, National Delegate from Azerbaijan to International Society for the History of Medicine (ISHM).

Dr. Alakbarli spent twenty years as a research scientist at the Institute of Manuscripts in Baku. Subsequently, he worked as an expert at the Centre of Sociological Studies in the Parliament of Azerbaijan (1993-1994). Professor Alakbarli gave seminars at the Institute of Manuscripts and at the Futurology University (Baku). He organized courses, specifically in the areas of study of medicinal plants and history of medicine.

Farid Alakbarli studied history culture and science in the Middle East and Azerbaijan. These studies were carried out on the basis of medieval Turkish, Arabic, and Persian manuscripts of the tenth through eighteenth centuries. He studied ancient medical manuscripts of Azerbaijan. As a result, 724 species of medicinal plants, 150 species of animals, 115 species of minerals, and 866 types of complex medicines used during the Middle Ages have been identified. The concept of health protection that existed in medieval Azerbaijan has been identified and studied for the first time.

Alakbarli is a historian researching medical manuscripts. He is the author of about 150 scientific and educational articles and twelve books. His contributions are on the history of science, culture, and medicine in Southern Europe and the Middle East.

DR. FARAH ALIYEVA is a specialist in the history of twentieth-century Azerbaijani music and began her professional activities in 1984 in research, teaching, and the promotion of music. A professor at the Baku Music Academy, author of several monographs, sourcebooks, anthologies and tutorials, as well as more than one hundred articles in periodicals, Dr. Aliyeva is well known in Azerbaijan for making music more accessible through her festival initiatives and numerous appearances on TV programs and at preconcert talks.

HANNAH BYERS is associate director at the BMW Guggenheim Lab of the Solomon R. Guggenheim Foundation. She rejoined the Solomon R. Guggenheim Museum in 2010 as Associate Director of Exhibition Management and in 2012 assumed overall project management for the BMW Guggenheim Lab, a mobile laboratory exploring the future of cities, traveling to nine major cities worldwide over six years.

Hannah has worked on feasibility and concept-development studies for museum projects around the world, assembling teams of scholars and specialists to develop museum programs and consulting on various aspects of architectural space programs, site analyses, as well as urban and legal infrastructures. In addition, she has worked on nearly seventy major international exhibitions in varying capacities, ranging from curator, researcher, and consultant to manager.

Before rejoining the Guggenheim, Hannah worked at GCAM (Global Cultural Asset Management) Group as Director of International Projects. In her previous tenure at the Guggenheim (2005-2008), Hannah worked as exhibitions manager and project manager. Prior to that, she was a curatorial assistant at The Phillips Collection in Washington, DC, and educational director of the American Academy of Foreign Languages in Moscow.

She is a contributing author and editor to numerous publications, including *Impressionist Still Life* (Abrams, 2001), *Georges Rouault at Work* (Phillips Collection, 2004), and *Reinterpreting Revolutionary Russia: Essays in Honour of James D. White* (Palgrave, Macmillan, 2006).

Hannah Byers received her PhD in Russian and East European studies from the University of Glasgow, her MA in museum studies from the University of Leicester, and her BA in history and humanities from the University of North Carolina at Asheville.

NICOLAS V. ILJINE was born in Paris in 1944. After studies in France and Great Britain, Iljine moved to Germany and later specialized in public relations. He has held various positions with Lufthansa Airlines, last as head of Worldwide Public Affairs, The Solomon R. Guggenheim Foundation, and the Global Cultural Asset Management Group in New York. At the Guggenheim Foundation he was involved in museum projects in Bilbao, Berlin, and Abu Dhabi. Iljine currently works as a consultant for several museums and cultural institutions in Europe. He organized such major exhibitions such as *The Great Utopia, Chagall's Jewish Theater, Amazons of the Avant-Garde,* and *Kazimir Malevich, Suprematism, and Russia!,* as well as shows devoted to Russian contemporary art in Miami. Among his works as an author or editor are *Sold Treasures of Russia,* Trilistnik, Moscow, 2000; *Odessa Memories,* University of Washington Press, 2003; *Pass to Paradise,* Vagrius, Moscow, 2008; *Nikolai Suetin,* Palace Editions, St. Petersburg, 2008. He is a founding member of the board of trustees of Kandinsky Prize and an honorary member of the Russian Academy of Arts. In 2006, Iljine was awarded the Order of Friendship by Russian President V. V. Putin.

JAHANGIR SELIMKHANOV has a professional background in musicology and music promotion. He has contributed to numerous cultural events and projects covering various art disciplines and spheres of cultural action (cultural policy, contemporary visual arts, museum work) in Azerbaijan and abroad. Selimkhanov has lectured and reported at universities, international symposia, workshops, and conferences in Oslo, Gothenburg, Tbilisi, Vienna, Cologne, Delhi, Thessaloniki, Newcastle, Riga, Bangkok, Zurich, Seoul, Kassel, Lisbon, Strasbourg, and Lviv. He is cofounder of Yeni Musiqi–Society for Contemporary Music (1995) and a member of the European Cultural Parliament (since 2005).